Planned & Unplanned:
Creative Handwoven Clothing

By

Pat White & Isa Vogel

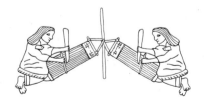

DOS TEJEDORAS FIBER ARTS PUBLICATIONS
SAINT PAUL, MINNESOTA

"The effectiveness of a garment must be partially gauged in social, magical and aesthetic terms which in some cases outweigh the practical functions of the clothing."

Crossroads of Continents
Catalog to an exhibition held at the Museum of Natural History, New York, NY; published by the Smithsonian Institution, September, 1988.

Edited by Karen Searle
Designed by Patrick Redmond
Garment sketches by Pat White and Laura Laurelli
Additional illustrations by Patrick Redmond
Color photos by Pat White
Black & white photos by Karen Searle and Patrick Redmond
Computer production by Claudia Debner
Editorial consultant Susan Larson Fleming
Weaving consultant and production assistant Margaret Miller

Front Cover photos: *Jigsaw Jacket* by Pat White; *Mohair Jacket* by Isa Vogel

Published by Karen L. Searle
Dos Tejedoras Fiber Arts Publications
757 Raymond Avenue
Saint Paul, Minnesota 55114

ISBN 0-932394-17-5

Library of Congress No. 92-071655

TABLE OF CONTENTS

ACKNOWLEDGEMENTS

The people who have lived with me during my seventeen years as a weaver deserve more than thanks. I'm sure my husband, Tom, didn't know what he was getting into when he gave me my first loom for Christmas one year. He and our sons, Jake and Ben, have been understanding and supportive despite missed dinners and neglected housework. Frequently they have been helpful critics. Most important, they have understood that just because I was at home didn't mean I wasn't a working person.

I have learned about weaving from my fellow weavers, my teachers and from my students. One of the greatest rewards of pursuing my interest in weaving clothing is being part of the large community of weavers and fiber artists.

A most wonderful by-product of weaving is the fellowship of weavers. In the fifteen years I have been weaving there have been many, many special people whose patience and kindness have been so happily shared. I want to say thank you to these friends and teachers.

To Albertje (Appie) Koopman who I think put woven clothing into the world as style; to Betty Oldenberg, of The Spinnery where I learned to weave; to Kerry Adams and her assistant, Lynn Brandt, of Fibre Crafts who gave me countless hints; to Howard and Marion Slepian; to Amalia, my patient pal of aba Wordprocessing Services; to Louise Laurelli for her drawings. I thank Phuouc Nuyen for her wondrous sewing, and Debbie Linden for weaving the wedding dress yardage. Last, but never least, my thanks to Marilyn Hirsh and Genny Minton.

The weaving guilds I belong to are the North Jersey Weavers and Jockey Hollow Weavers (NJ) and they too have given me great encouragement along the way. I am indebted to Arlene Levine for using the perfect word combinations to start me on my way to my first weaving lessons.

Special thanks to my husband, Sandy, and our kids, Robin, and Andy, who have always encouraged me.

Pat White

Isa Vogel

*There are two kinds of people
in this world...*

We'd like to introduce ourselves – one of each kind. We are Pat White and Isa Vogel, and our creative outlet is making handwoven clothing. We have enjoyed "talking shop" with one another off and on since we met over ten years ago. We admire each other's work and find it innovative and wonderful to wear; but what has continued to intrigue us is the completely different way we go about creating our garments. From the very first glimmer of an idea to the finished garment, our routes are as far apart as they could be. One of us starts with a well-detailed map and travels a reasonably straight road with few detours. The other meanders and makes a lot of design decisions enroute.

In our conversations about the way we work, we have discovered that each of us makes hundreds of choices – some good, some not-so-good – on the way to a finished piece. We thought it would be encouraging and perhaps even liberating to share how we work, including the high and low points. Perhaps other weavers will identify with the process and 'creative personality' that seems most familiar to them, and realize that creativity is just a series of small steps that everyone can take, using the style that works best for them!

To show how we work, we assigned ourselves four broadly defined projects, and recorded the details of our progress and pitfalls. We met regularly to compare our progress, and then compiled plans, notes, and conversations about these projects: how we came to the idea; what decisions we made along the way; how we felt about the garments as we worked on them and when they were finished; and whether we were satisfied with them. This book is the record of working through those clothing projects.

To emphasize the contrast in our styles of working, the page layouts in this book are more formal and planned for Pat's projects and more informal and impulsive for Isa's.

We value creativity; we hope you will use these projects as a starting point for your own handwoven clothing designs.

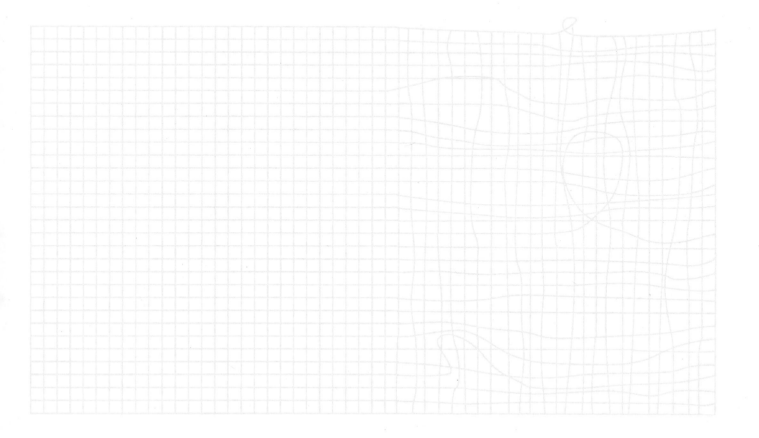

Pat White at work in her home studio.

My mother decided that I could use the sewing machine when I was in the fourth grade. The first thing I made was a green, black, and white rayon dress. It had a full skirt with patch pockets gathered onto a fitted bodice, with set-in sleeves and a horseshoe neckline which enclosed a white piqué dickey. There was a zipper and buttons and buttonholes. (I have always loved a challenge!) Mother showed me how to use the machine, but she let me teach myself and never told me my project was too difficult. I wore this dress proudly. I don't remember how good a job it was, but I had a very positive feeling about it. After that, I did a lot of sewing. To me it was an acceptable way of showing off.

A logical choice for my college education was nearby Cornell University's College of Home Economics, where I majored in textiles and clothing. I took clothing construction and design courses, as well as figure drawing; I gained enough facility to sketch my ideas clearly.

I toyed with the idea of a career in retailing in New York City after graduation, but was offered a Masters in Education Program fellowship which was too good to refuse. Then it was marriage to a law student and a teaching job to support us.

On a trip to Williamsburg, Virginia in 1974, a visit to the weaving house reminded me that I had often thought about making my own cloth. I signed up for a weaving course on my return home. Since then I have been weaving clothing.

After moving to New Jersey in 1976 and finding other weavers, I concentrated on improving my skills and began showing and selling my own designs. Soon I was being asked to lecture and teach, and I sold all that I could produce. Now I divide my time between a limited production line and as many one-of-a-kind pieces as I can manage. My favorite client is one who gives me a general idea of what she wants (maybe color and occasion) and asks to see what I can come up with.

I have been lecturing and teaching workshops on handwoven clothing since 1980 and have observed that the two approaches Isa and I represent typify the extremes of a continuum on which each creative person has a place. Few people find themselves in the middle of this continuum; most tend either toward an intuitive, somewhat ad hoc style, or toward a more intellectual approach in which planning plays a bigger part. We think both ways are the "right way."

Many people are unsure of their own creativity and ability to get an idea and carry it out. People compare themselves to others and when they see only the results, that can be intimidating. But in fact, everyone can, and does, go about creating one step at a time. Thinking about the *process* instead of the daunting task of producing a smashing product can provide the courage to begin. With experience we make better decisions, and our woven garments begin to look better and better. People compliment us, but more importantly, we are excited about our own work. This is what creativity is – a process, not a product.

Why is a woman like me a weaver? I am impatient, impulsive, and impetuous. It's an impossibility to follow recipes, maps or directions of any kind. It is tedious to do as directed, and infinitely more interesting to leap and then look!

Why begin if the outcome is known? I am frequently immersed in chaos and the process of extricating myself produces wonderful surprises. Serendipity is magical! When I began weaving garments I was attracted to the excitement of unknown endings.

Fiber has been a constant presence in my life. My grandmother and mother were talented needlewomen whose works I treasure. They did try to entice me to do it, but it was not an activity for a kid who wouldn't color within the lines. They sat for hours doing their handwork; I still marvel at their patience. As much as I appreciated their work, I had no interest in learning to do it.

Escape was no longer possible when I entered 8th grade home economics. The cooking curriculum was difficult enough, having to measure ingredients exactly; but sewing was my undoing. We girls had to make our graduation dresses. I learned quickly that the sewing machine loathed me as much as I loathed it! The dress was finally completed with the peplum askew, and the teacher with more grey hairs in June than she had in September. Fortunately, she and I were spared the embarassment of my wearing the dress. I had ptomaine poisoning on graduation day!

This was, I had hoped, my last brush with the fabric world. My dreams were for a publishing career and after college I worked briefly in publishing until I married a law student and my career changed to teaching in order to support us.

About this time a dear friend gave me a crewel embroidery kit. She thought it would amuse me while my husband studied, and rather than hurt her feelings, I finished it. The discipline drove me to distraction; yet the yarns and colors fascinated me.

Over the years I tried stitchery, needlepoint, batik, and tie dyeing, but these weren't satisfying. I wanted to explore further. Hearing of a nearby weaving studio, I enrolled in a class. My life has not been the same since. When I saw the yarns draped every which way over the loom to later emerge as fabric, I was hooked. I learned the demands imposed by the loom. Just as I must obey traffic laws, I know that I have to obey the loom's rules. After taking various classes, I wanted to concentrate on woven clothing. How to accomplish this when I can't and won't sew?

Isa Vogel in one of her impetuous moments.

The solution was loom-shaped clothing, or so I thought. But I was always in some kind of predicament, short of warp, weft, width, length, or sometimes all of the above! At first I would throw the fabric away, and many times I was tempted to throw the loom with it! I was always shocked to see how utterly different the garment looked as it came from the loom. (Nothing like what I had planned). After many, many of these experiments, the next time it happened I stood there and hollered "Now what?" That "Now what" became the mental shove to create a solution. It was apparent that what is perverse in me created the problems and what is perverse in me could also create the clothes. The magic that worked elsewhere in my life could be applied to weaving. Designing intuitively doesn't always guarantee that you'll like the finished design, but by using intuitive ingenuity you can turn a coat into a sweater, or a jacket into a coat; the problem is the solution and this, for me is the beginning.

Pat and Isa:

Introductions accomplished, it is certainly clear which of us is the planner and which the crisis response weaver. The garment descriptions that follow are not meant to be exact recipes for reproducing each item. They are descriptive of the problem-solving process in weaving successful garments, and we hope they are helpful in providing some practical how-to details as well. Tips on sewing with handwoven fabrics, adding knitted trims to handwovens and rainbow dyeing are a few of the subjects included in the appendices.

Our assignments were a jacket, a woven sweater, an evening ensemble and a lightweight coat. These are typical garments that handweavers make. It is not surprising, given our opposite approaches, that we had great difficulty agreeing even on these limitations!

Our first project, a jacket, was to be lightweight and unlined. We forged ahead to unknown trials, tribulations, and successes.

Planned Pat's Jigsaw Jacket

Design Process

The first step is the idea. Ideas always evolve, even the ones that seem to pop into your head fully formed. For me it takes time for me to get good ideas. I usually need to put myself into the circumstances where ideas come most easily. I need to sit down with a pencil to sketch. I might have a vague mental image of what I want to weave, but it would be impossible for me to get from the idea to the loom without drawing it first. Drawing forces me to make many choices about how the pattern pieces will be shaped, how they will fit together, how they will be adapted to the rectangular woven format, and where the design focus will be. Details like closings, neckline, or cuffs can be resolved, or partially resolved in the sketch. Then I evaluate the sketch. Does it motivate me to do the weaving?

The *Jigsaw Jacket* evolved from several directions. I had been teaching a weave-drafting class and we had just covered 8-harness twills. I had an idea for a pieced jacket woven in several different treadlings of an 8-harness point threading, each a different color weft on a black warp. I had a large supply of 2-ply shetland wool for the warp and 2-ply wool tweed for the weft. I had used this combination in previous jackets, but this time I decided the jacket would not have facings or hems. Instead I intended to felt the fabric to a greater degree in the finishing. Sampling was still necessary, but confined to finding the degree of felting needed and the best join for the seams.

A second source for the design was a lecture I had been preparing on "Getting Away from the Rectangular in Handwoven Clothing." One suggestion I made in the lecture was to shape the pattern pieces, introducing curves instead of straight seams. The jacket I was planning would be a good illustration for both the class and the lecture. Somewhere in the recesses of my mind, the idea of fitting curved shapes together like jigsaw pieces emerged. A linen jacket by Christian Lacroix in the *New York Times Fashions of the Times* may also have influenced the design. A reading of the current fashion scene ruled out the recent oversized look in favor of a shorter, more fitted jacket.

Warp Plan

Working from my sketch, I saw that I needed five different colors and five different twill patterns. I lined up cones of yarn in different combinations and settled on burgundy, deep blue, dark brown, gold, and gray. One sleeve would be two-pieced, the other one piece and a different color. To reinforce the asymmetry and the jigsaw idea, the closure would be interlocking shapes in a yin-yang variation (Figs. 1.1, 1.2A and 1.2B).

Materials

Warp:
2-ply Shetland wool *(Harrisville)*
   black

Weft:
2-ply Wool Tweed *(Harrisville)*
   Burgundy
   Curry
   Granite
   Indigo
   Timber

Sett:
10 e.p.i.

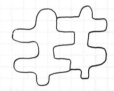

1.1. Interlocking jigsaw shapes.

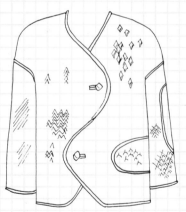

1.2A. Jacket front.

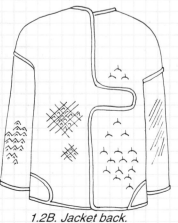

1.2B. Jacket back.

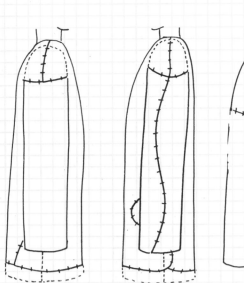

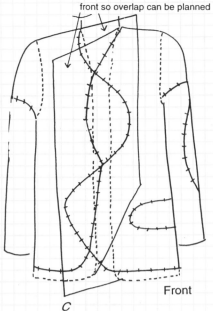

Extra muslin added to each side front so overlap can be planned

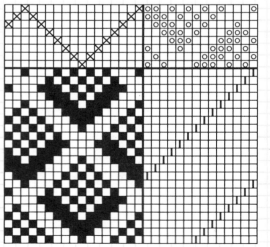

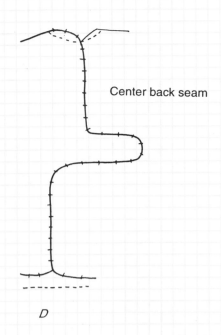

Center back seam

Right side
A

Left side
B

C

Front

D

1.3A-D. To alter pattern for a jigsaw design:
1. Cut original pattern in muslin and baste together (no hems or facings needed).
2. Draw new seam lines on the original muslin with pen or marker. (Add extra muslin to each front to accommodate overlap.)
3. Cut out the new pattern pieces:
a) lay the new muslin pieces on pattern paper .
b) trace around the new pieces, refining and trueing where necessary.
4. Cut a new pattern with no seam allowances, hems, or facings.

Garment Pattern

To make a pattern for the jacket, I began working in muslin from a simple jacket in my pattern collection. I sewed *Butterick 9530,* with a long stitch, using no facings or hems, and then drew the new "jigsaw" seam lines on the muslin jacket. I cut along these new seam lines and, using a new piece of muslin, made a new pattern by drawing around the cut pieces, adding on dropped shoulder extensions and refining the seamlines where necessary. The dropped-shoulder sleeve required the most change. I cut on the new seam lines and cut off any old seam allowances where I needed to, since I decided to butt the pattern pieces and sew them together with a decorative figure-8 join in black. This would be a major design element, outlining the jigsaw shapes. I butted the new muslin

A

B

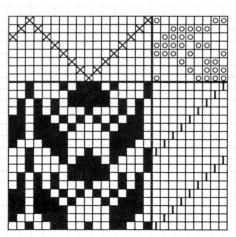

1.5. Draft.

1.6 A-E. Treadling variations used with draft in fig. 1.5.

6

Shapes of new pattern pieces

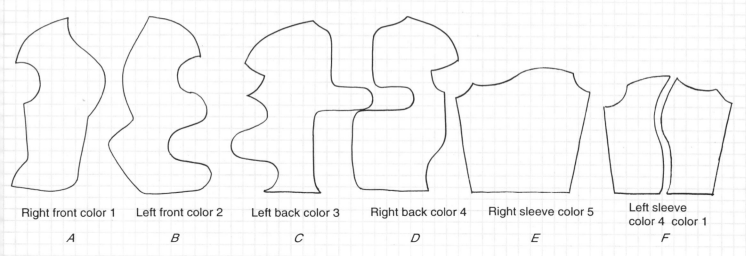

Right front color 1	Left front color 2	Left back color 3	Right back color 4	Right sleeve color 5	Left sleeve color 4 color 1
A	B	C	D	E	F

pattern pieces together with a broad running zigzag stitch to catch both pieces. Then I tried it on for fit and style. (See Figs. 1.3 A-D and 1.4 A-F.)

Sampling and Weaving

Once I determined the size and shape of the pattern pieces, I was ready to decide on the warp width that would be necessary, using the widest part of the jacket back and half-sleeve combinations. I also had to decide the total warp length and the length of each color area to be woven. At this point, I wove a sample to determine shrinkage. I decided to allow for 20% shrinkage in the width and 20% in the length. An advantage of cutting and sewing over loom-shaping is that these calculations need not be exact as long as enough is allowed, since the pattern will be cut from the cloth.

1.4.A-F. Shapes of new pattern pieces. Make a second muslin model using the new pattern pieces to check for accuracy of seams and for fit. Butt pieces together using a wide running zigzag stitch.

C

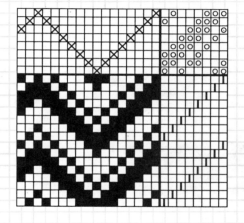

D

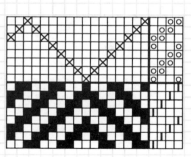

E

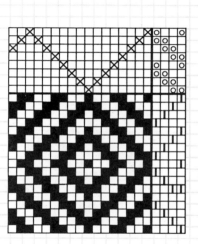

Warp Plan

Curry 19"
    Right sleeve
    Color 5

Indigo 30"
    Left front
    Color 2

Granite 30"
    Left sleeve
    Color 1

    Right front
    Color 1

Burgundy 30"
    Right back
    Color 4

    Left sleeve
    Color 4

Timber 30"
    Left back
    Color 2

26"

1.7. Pattern layout on warp.

One of the twill patterns I wished to weave (Fig. 1.6 A) required more than my 10 treadles, so I had to figure out a way to combine treadles using both feet to achieve it. Since I needed less than one yard, it was not overly demanding to complete that much fabric using an awkward treadling. The arrangement of pattern pieces and order of weaving the twill variations are shown in Fig. 1.7.

Fabric Finishing

I finished the fabric by zigzag stitching the ends and machine washing the fabric for 6 minutes in warm water on the normal cycle, with gentle agitation. I put it in the dryer on low for about 5 minutes, then hung it on a rack to finish drying, supporting at one-yard intervals. I gave it a light pressing before pinning on the pattern pieces and cutting. I cut out the pattern according to Fig. 1.7.

1.8. Back view of the Jigsaw Jacket.

Garment Assembly

My goal was to have flat, flexible, butted seams that emphasized the design. The major problem in construction was preventing distortion of the edges. After cutting, I handled the pieces very carefully, immediately using a running zigzag stitch on all edges. This distorted the edges, but it was possible to steam-press them flat again. I then butted the edges of each piece together with a running zigzag stitch. The next step, a result of doing several samples of my intended seam join, was to determine how wide the figure-8 stitch was to be – 5/8" – and machine-stitch a line just over 1/4" from each edge to have a firm foundation to embroider around. Otherwise, with the twill structure, I couldn't get the appearance of a straight edge on the join. I worked the figure-8 stitch with the 2-ply Shetland wool, placing stitches close enough to completely cover the twill fabric. A slight rippling still resulted, which I remedied by using a running stitch with the Shetland, hidden under each side of the join, and pulling this until taut to ease the fabric into a flat, neat join. See Figs.1.9A-C. (Where there's a will, there's a way.)

Figure-8 Join

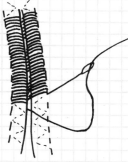

1.9A. Running zigzag along raw edge. Note line of machine stitching just over 1/4" from the edge.

1.9B. Figure 8 stitches made densely with Shetland wool, covering the fabric completely.

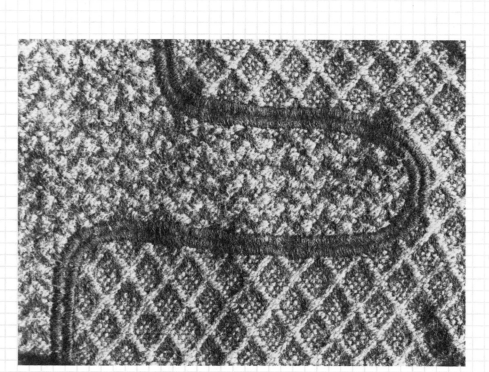

1.10. Detail of handstitched join.

1.9C. Ending join. Running stitch of Shetland wool hidden beneath embroidery join on each side and pulled taut to eliminate distortion.

Edging

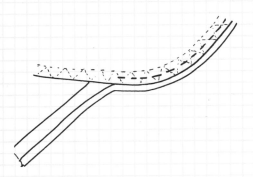

1.11A. Purchased cotton bias-covered cording cut to 3/8" wide.

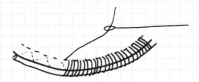

1.11B. Cording applied to edge with zipper foot, stretching cording slightly as it is sewn.

1.11C. Corded edge overcast with shetland wool, densely enough to cover the fabric completely.

The neck, sleeve, and hem edges presented another stitching problem which had to be solved in a different way. I trimmed purchased cotton bias-covered cording to the appropriate 3/8" width. I stretched the cording slightly as I applied it to the right side of the edge; it reinforced the edge and maintained the shape. I then overcast the edge with the 2-ply Shetland wool, taking care not to pull it too tightly, to avoid curling the edge. See Figs. 1.11A-C.

Finishing Touches

I cut the buttonholes, then reinforced and overcast them. Fig. 1.12 shows the closure. As a final touch, I inserted shoulder pads. A steam pressing, using a cloth, finished the jacket.

Comments

The handstitched joins and overcast edges on this jacket were very time-consuming, but not difficult to do. Another edging method, which I intend to try on a similarly styled hooded coat, uses bias wool jersey binding. This jacket was included in the fashion show at the *Convergence '88* conference of the Handweavers Guild of America.

1.12. Detail of jacket closure.

MATERIALS LIST

Warp:
Mohair (Stanley Berocco)

Weft:
mixed yarns, including:
Donegal Homespun (Tahki)
space-dyed mohair
rayon chenille (Silk City)

Sett:
8 e.p.i.

Design Process

Chanukah was coming and my daughter Robin wanted a jacket from "Mums." I decided to make our first book project for her.

Many times the yarns themselves are my main inspiration for a fabric. My loom room is a harmonious clutter of yarns covering every inch of space not occupied by looms. They are arranged by color, texture, or grouped for possible future inspiration, but sometimes I find their beauty intimidating. What weave structure, what garment could possibly enhance their loveliness?

Grey is one of my favorite colors, and it also happens to match my daughter's eyes. I had limited quantities of a grey mohair and a wool, which I had space-dyed and could not be replicated exctly. (See Appendix 5 for dyeing information.) Nevertheless, I wanted to use them. If I used both yarns, there might be enough for a short, light-weight jacket.

The textures and colors suggested a soft, romantic style and I chose to add full, knitted sleeves to enhance the mood.

As I thought more about about it, I wanted the jacket design to focus on the closure. As every weaver knows, closures can make or break a garment. I reviewed every closure I had ever used and none seemed suitable. A straight edge seemed too harsh for these soft materials; an undulating line might work well. This thinking process led me to consider using a tapestry panel on an asymmetrical jacket front. Snaps could be camouflaged under the tapestry's curved edges. To showcase the lush yarns, I selected a weave structure of 7/1 twill, loosely sett.

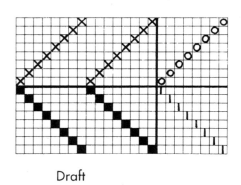

Draft

I threaded the mohair on an 8-harness loom to reduce the stickiness of the sheds.

Weaving

There was enough yarn for a three-yard, thirty-inch wide warp. I planned to use the warp width as the jacket length. I wove the 20 inches for the back first, then the front underpanel, and finished with the 17-inch right front tapestry panel. Intuition made me stop to feel the tapestry. It was too flimsy.

Now what!?"

Detour

Get rid of the tapestry immediately! When it was cut from the weaving, a piece 28" wide (lost 2 inches in weaving) and 40" in length was left. Also I found that the twill looked much prettier inside on the 1/7 side!

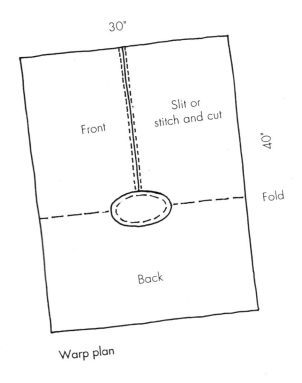

Warp plan

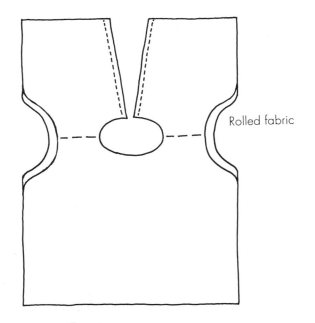

Top view

A Garment Evolves

I folded the twill fabric in half and stay-stitched it to mark a center seam and neck opening. Often, when I am in a predicament such as this I go to the mirror and then drape the fabric over me. This usually offers a natural solution. I saw that the sides overlapped quite nicely, but this left the back too wide. An inverted pleat would solve that. Still, the shoulders and front were too wide, and I tried rolling the extra width. The roll at the shoulders would not stay rounded when I sewed it, but I liked that idea. At the local upholstery shop I found half-inch round cording. I rolled the fabric around the cord and blind-stitched it securely. It worked perfectly, showing the fabric's reverse side as a bonus, providing a contrast with the body of the jacket.

Knitted Sleeves

I knit sleeves for the jacket out of the leftover warp and weft yarns. It is important to blend the yarns to integrate the weaving and knitting. (See Appendix 8 for knitting hints.)

Back view of jacket with inverted pleat.

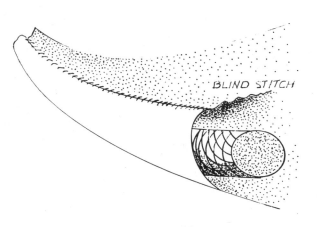

Cording inserted at armhole edge for rolled trim.

Blending colors. When winding the shuttles to weave the jacket body, I wind bobbins with different lengths of three different yarns wound together. When one yarn runs out, I splice on another. This does away with any regular color patterns and adds quite a bit of sparkle. I used the same idea of blending for the knitting yarns, combining three or four of the weft/warp yarns and used large needles for the knitting (size 11-13).

Finishing Touches

For a bias tape edging, using the same blend of yarns I knitted a bias strip wide enough to cover the front edges and the bottom of the jacket.

Comments

When my detour was completed and I asked myself, "Was it worth it?" I was satisfied. This jacket seemed totally integrated in both style and yarn.

Knitted Sleeves

Cast on for the 22" circumference armholes as determined from your gauge. Knit in stockinette until 5 1/2 inches from your desired length. At this time, drastically decrease stitches over next 2-3 or 4 rows and then change to needles 2-3 sizes smaller and knit a 5 1/2" cuff in stockinette or ribbing. Sew the finished sleeve to the armhole.

I think a smoother look is obtained by using stockinette stitch instead of ribbing at the cuffs.

Knit Bias Tape Edging

To knit a bias tape, cast on stitches for the desired width and knit the first row, increasing one stitch at the beginning of the row. Knit to within 2 stitches of the end, and knit these last 2 stitches together. Purl the next row. Repeat, and continue alternating knit and purl rows to the desired length.

No Loose Ends Pat's Coat

Design Process

I mentioned my favorite kind of customer in the introduction. One of these treasured types came to me for a coat that she could wear over a number of dresses she owned. These dresses were all silky textures and spring colors – pastel pinks and blues on predominantly white grounds. One dress was striped, another floral, and there were abstract and geometric prints as well as solid colors.

The challenge was to design a coat that would work with this wide variety of fabrics and yet stand on its own. The easy solution would have been to choose a solid color, or a weave and yarn combination that would give the impression of a solid color. Yet my client and I wanted the coat to be a Pat White design with the graphic element that characterizes my handwoven clothing, but which could coexist with the printed patterns of the dresses.

It's fun to work out a one-of-a-kind design with a customer. I like to get as much input as possible, so that in some ways it is a joint creation. I often start by showing some fabric samples and yarns. My yarns are stored floor to ceiling in a 12-foot wall, and most people can't resist an invitation to begin picking among the colors and textures. In fact, the problem is not in getting clients involved with the yarns, but in keeping their mind on the project at hand.

Often when I am designing a garment for someone else, it helps if I can get them to come up with a word to define the look or feeling they want. "Elegant" was the operative word for this design. We wanted a slightly fitted shape, definitely not a large flowing garment. It would have a simple, unstructured, yet dressy look, with set-in sleeves. Because of the dress styles that were to be worn under the coat, we decided on a cardigan front with pockets. (Pockets are an almost universal request, and something that much handwoven clothing lacks.)

Working together helps clarify ideas for both of us and helps ensure that the end result will be what the client wants. Some people have difficulty visualizing a finished garment, so I always do a sketch (Fig. 2.1). At the same time, I try to explain that I am presenting a general idea which may change somewhat as I experiment with materials, weaves, and pattern design.

Because my client is short, we decided on a somewhat vertical emphasis in the weave, broken by an ombre band of colors which she had chosen. This shaded band of color would be placed at the hem, and for an unexpected detail, there would be an asymmetric placement of this band at the yoke and sleeves. We decided against several other options such as strong vertical stripes of color and an all-over plaid.

Materials

Warp:
A mixture of cotton, rayon and silk, in whites and off whites including:
Contessa silk/rayon *(Silk City)*
Afrique Cotton *(Scott's)*
a rayon novelty ply
a silk noil

Weft:
The Contessa blend alternating with a bundle of the other three warp yarns, either in the white mix, or in shades of blue, pink and lavender ombre.

Sett:
15 e.p.i.

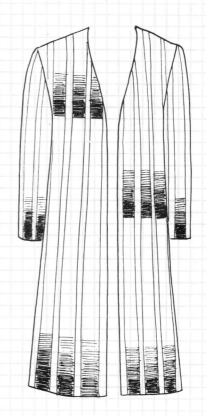

2.1. *Coat.*

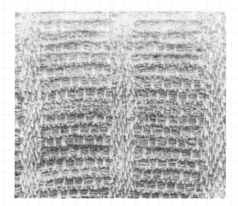

2.2. Detail of fabric.

Warp Plan

My client chose a variety of yarns for the warp – whites of different fibers, textures, and tones. We mixed white cotton flake, white cotton and shiny rayon ply, off-white silk noil, off-white cotton flake, and white rayon and silk blend. I set these closely enough to get a mostly-white stripe in the sateen weave areas (Fig. 2.2).

I used a silk-rayon blend yarn for every-other weft pick (the tabby in the overshot areas) alternating with a bundle of three threads used as one – the off-white cotton flake, the white silk rayon blend, and the white cotton and shiny rayon ply. In the ombre areas, the same types of yarns were bundled, but the colors gradually changed, one thread at a time, from blues and lavender, to blues, to lighter blues, to blues and pinks, to pinks, to pinks and white, to whites. The tabby single weft also changed from blue to pink to white.

Sampling

Once the basic idea was agreed upon, I began to experiment with the weave. It was necessary to sample this fabric to see if the mixed warp would cause shrinkage problems, to check for color fastness, and to assess the sett and hand of the fabric.

To accomplish the appearance of a band of color and texture with superimposed white verticals, I threaded sateen weave stripes of varied

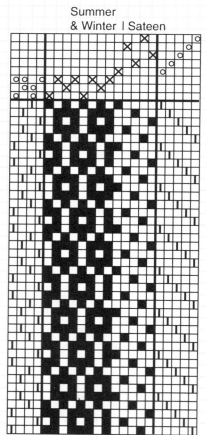

Summer
& Winter | Sateen

Treadle
with left foot

Treadle
with right foot

2.3. Threading and treadling: stripes of sateen alternate with wider stripes of the summer and winter block, random widths.

2.4. Coat front.

widths, alternating with a 3-thread overshot (which could also be thought of as one block of a summer and winter weave), Fig. 2.3. Since sateen is easier to weave raising one harness instead of four, I opted to weave the cloth face down. To accomplish this combination of weaves would require 40 treadles on my 12-treadle loom! A simple solution was to use one foot to treadle for the sateen and the other foot to treadle for the overshot. This way, one foot could progressively treadle 1,2,3,4,5 and the other foot produce the overshot on 6,7,8 and 9. Fortunately, the first sample was satisfactory. I was ready to go ahead with the weaving as soon as I made a muslin pattern for the coat, which I needed to determine yardage.

Garment Pattern

Generally, I adapt a commercial sewing pattern rather than draft one from scratch. In this case, I used the same basic jacket pattern as for the *Jigsaw Jacket.* I took from it the shoulder line, the sleeves and armhole. I lengthened it to coat dimensions, added pockets in the side seams, and recut the cardigan front slightly. A facing was cut for the neck and front edge. See Fig. 2.4. Fig. 2.5 shows a detail of the coat back.

The weave plan for the pattern pieces is shown in Fig. 2.6. Note that extra fabric has been included for facings. Fig. 2.7 shows how to add pockets in the side seam.

Weaving Layout

Weave borders at each end in white for hem facings and seams before starting ombre band.

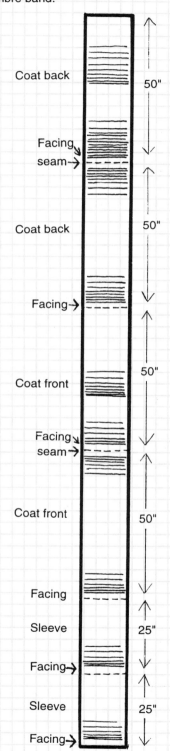

Coat back — 50"

Facing
seam →

Coat back — 50"

Facing →

Coat front — 50"

Facing
seam →

Coat front — 50"

Facing

Sleeve — 25"

Facing →

Sleeve — 25"

Facing →

2.6. Weaving layout: Warp is 15" wide and 250" long.

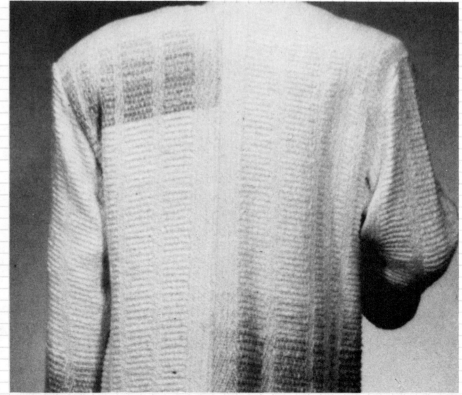

2.5. Coat back.

17

Adding Pockets

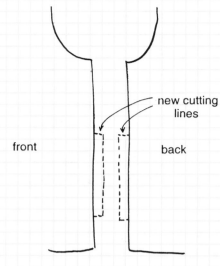

front   new cutting lines   back

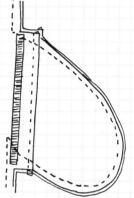

8"   10"

← 5" →

To add pockets in a side seam:

1. Redraw side seams, front and back, adding a 1" to 1 1/2" extension, 8" long at a point comfortable for your arm. The extension is important so that the pocket seam is invisible.

2. Cut a pocket from lining fabric. Cut 2 pieces for each pocket.

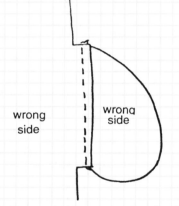

wrong side   wrong side

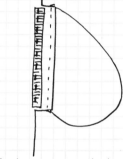

3. Sew pocket to seam extension front. Repeat for back.

4. For loose or stretchy handwovens, stitch seam tape just outside of seam line to stabilize.

5. Stitch the coat seams and pocket pieces together – right sides together.

2.7. Adding pockets to a side seam.

Garment Assembly

I cut out the garment pieces and immediately zigzagged the edges to prevent raveling. I assembled the pieces according to the pattern instructions. This coat was sewn using standard clothing construction techniques, with some adaptations for handwoven material. In addition to adding pockets to a side seam, there are a number of other dressmaking and tailoring techniques that are particularly helpful when sewing handwoven garments. Several of the most useful, such as tips for making hems invisible, have been included in Appendix 2.

Comments

This coat fits my client and her wardrobe well and is a very versatile garment.

Loose Ends Isa's Coat

MATERIALS

Warp:
Wools (Wilde Yarns)
Tumbleweed
Pebbles

Weft:
Heavy wool (Henry's Attic)
Periwinkle
Toros II

Sett:
6 e.p.i.

Design Process

An unnatural phenomenon occurs when I wear scarves. By some invisible means of locomotion they march off my neck never to be seen again. They are most likely littering parking lots, driveways and theatres, probably having a reunion with my gloves. Since I am well beyond the age of tethering scarves to my coats, I began to think of a solution through weaving.

Although I had always woven them separately, I now wanted scarf and coat attached together through a loom-shaped method. I could picture the neck area and the drape of a scarf. It seemed logical to extend a section of warp at the front of the coat's neckline for the scarf. Since my loom is 54" wide, I decided to use the loom width as the coat length with an extension for the scarf at one end. (See Appendix 6 for details on adding an extension to a warp.)

I chose muted colors of minimally-textured wools, plus a silk-and-wool combination to be woven on a plain weave threading.

False Start

When I began to measure the warp, there was not enough yarn for a full length coat; instead I decided on a car coat of 30" length. It wove off quite easily until I reached the scarf extension. Weaving at the one extreme side of the loom proved to be awkward.

After the coat was sewn, its finished look was much less than the sum of its parts. The weave structure did little to complement the style, as it was much too flat

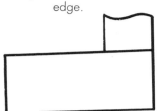

Coat Warp Plan 1
(First attempt with scarf at front neck edge.

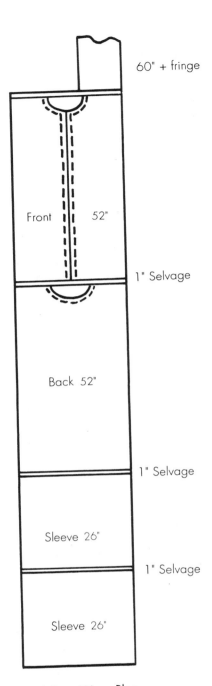

60" + fringe

Front 52"

1" Selvage

Back 52"

1" Selvage

Sleeve 26"

1" Selvage

Sleeve 26"

Final Coat Warp Plan

for the sumptuous style I had wanted. Also the scarf coming off at the front of the neck draped oddly. Now 𝖂𝖍𝖆𝖙?

Detour

Off to the mirror for an intensive critique. Looking at the jacket on me, I was bewildered as to how I had even arrived at this garment. The style I had originally envisioned was lush, yet this was flat! The zipper closure was awkward and the colors looked trite though I had really liked all the yarns when I began. All together, it was BAD. However, attaching a scarf to a coat still seemed a good idea.

A Garment Evolves

It was back to the loom room to rethink and redesign. I first changed the weave structure. In order to obtain a sumptuous fabric, fluffy yarns alone were not the answer. The effect had to come from the weave structure as well. I chose a 4-thread-mock leno from Ann Sutton's *The Structure of Weaving*. It's an open weave, and with billowy textured yarns, it would coordinate with the design.

Weaving order:
Weave both sleeves first.
Weave back to desired length.
Weave coat front from bottom up to length desired.
Weave scarf extension last.
At the same time you begin the scarf extension, weave the right shoulder selvage.
When that is completed, cut and tie the coat warp and continue with the scarf.

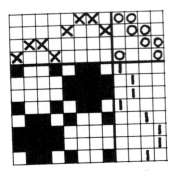

Draft

Detail coat with scarf.

My original warp plan had the weaving width used as the coat's length, and the scarf extension was off the side of the neck. This time I used the warp direction for the coat length. I extended the extra warp off the left shoulder, which was 10 inches wide. The scarf width is 9 inches. The coat front can be woven with two shuttles or stitched and cut.

In order to have a strong shoulder seam, I wove 1 1/2-inch selvages. A lot of weight hangs from the shoulders and the scarf adds even more weight. I needed the selvages as stabilizers for the rather loose weave.

This pattern is adaptable for a narrow loom by weaving the coat in strips of half the back's width.

Fabric Finishing

When I unrolled the new coat from the loom, I could see that the choice of weave and yarns were integrated – no surprises so far! There was a lot of shrinkage due to the loose weave and fulling of the fabric. I fulled it in the washing machine on gentle cycle for 2 minutes, and I omitted the spin cycle. I rolled the fabric up in towels to soak up the water and then put it in the dryer for 2-3 minutes. Then I hung it over the shower rod, continually rotating the fabric to avoid creases. The finished width was 26 inches.

Garment Assembly and Finishing Touches

To finish off the scarf, I knotted the fringe. The scarf could have been woven with different but related

Fabric sample

I think weaving the front with two shuttles is easier than machine stitching this fabric later. The fluffy yarns catch in the machine!

colors, or wound on with additional warp that could be woven and made into cuffs and/or a collar.

I sewed the coat side seams by hand and machine stitched the shoulders, using the selvages to hold the fabric firmly. The selvages enable the scarf to hang freely from its point of emanation. I added large shoulder pads and tapered the sleeve to avoid a lot of extra fabric weight. I worked one row of single crochet around the cuff to gather in the fullness. I machine stitched along the hemline and cut along it with pinking shears. I edged it with a row of single crochet in a fine yarn to cover the stitching.

Crochet Trim

For the sleeve and front trims, I made a band of double crochet with the fluffiest yarn and fulled it slightly by washing it in warm water and putting it in the dryer with a turkish towel on moderate heat. I checked it every couple of minutes, and when it was fluffy enough I let it air dry. I attached this band inside-out to the coat's front edges and used the same crochet trim inside and the outside of the cuffs. As a final touch, I sewed hooks and eyes under the trim.

Comments

I was happy that I persevered with this coat. The weave texture looks like popcorn. It's fun to wear, and very warm. Sometimes I wear the scarf wrapped as a stole, or as a hood pulled over my head.

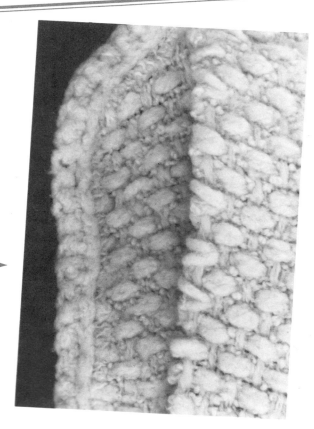

Detail of left coat front showing crocheted edging and scarf.

Sett Pat's Sweater

Design Process

The idea for this unusual sweater began, as did the idea for the *Jigsaw Jacket,* when I was exploring ways to think of woven clothing as something other than a construction of rectangles. One day when I was exploring in pattern books at a fabric store, a *Simplicity* pattern (#6899) for a bias-cut T-shirt caught my eye. The main pattern piece was a narrow rectangle which spiralled around the body, forming a tubular shape. I bought the pattern and filed it away. I used the idea a few years later for a jacket. As I was working on the jacket, it became apparent that the concept would work even better in a top that had no front opening to disturb the diagonal line.

The next step in the evolution of this design came when I developed it for use in a weaving class. I have often been asked to teach "handwoven clothing" to guild groups. Many people begin weaving because they want to make clothing. For those with some sewing experience, it can be just a few short steps to making successful woven clothing. Learning to make stable, drapable cloth is the first step; designing or choosing suitable patterns is a second; and adapting conventional sewing techniques to handwoven clothing is a third. People who sew have a good idea of how clothing hangs on the body, how darts work, how sleeves and collars are shaped, and how pieces fit together.

Handwoven cloth may be composed of yarns or threads of wider diameter than those in commercially available cloth, and some is woven more loosely. As a result, cutting, reinforcing, and seam finishing may have to be accomplished somewhat differently. Sewers can understand and adapt.

However, many others bring little but enthusiasm to a class in handwoven clothing – they are trying to learn weaving, clothing design, and construction all at once. I sought a way to involve everyone in a specific design problem, limiting the variables, so the class would appeal to beginners and experts. Everyone used the same one-color, plain-weave cotton warp and the same spiral-seamed pattern which is very easy to sew. It has only one long seam, two shoulder seams, two sleeves, and neck and hem finishes. This garment can be woven on 18" to 20"- wide looms. Everyone could focus on the design possibilities.

The designing can be done on a paper model using pencils or felt tip pens. It's something that's very interesting to do in paper because there is a kind of "aha" experience that occurs the first time everyone folds the pattern and sees how it goes together. Once the discovery is made that the diagonal seam will appear once in front and twice in back, and that by changing the neckline it can appear instead twice in front and only once in back, the design possibilities are increased. (See Figs. 3.1A and 3.1B.)

The beauty of this spiral-seamed design is that it forces thinking in a different way. We all know that designing clothing is a three-dimensional

Materials

Body:
Warp:
2-ply Shetland wool *(Harrisville)*
    black, peacock, royal, plum

Weft:
2-ply Tweed *(Harrisville)*
    granite
2-ply Shetland wool
    black

Sett:
10 e.p.i.

Sleeves:
Warp:
2-ply Shetland wool *(Harrisville)*
    black
Weft:
2-ply Shetland wool *(Harrisville)*
    peacock, royal

Sett:
12 e.p.i.

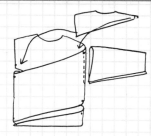

3.1A Spiral sweater schematic.

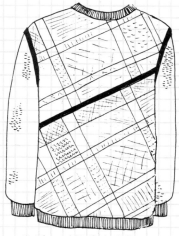

3.1A and B. Spiral Sweater.

3.2. Threading Drafts.
For body: Black dividing stripe (A) is 1 1/2" wide. Other blocks are 3", 4" and 6 1/2" wide. Whole draft repeated for total width with complete treadling sequence below.
For sleeves: Repeat Draft #A above for 24" width. Use threading IV.

Repeat between each block:

A

B

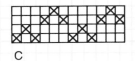

C

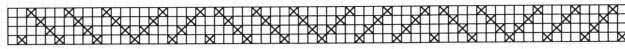

D

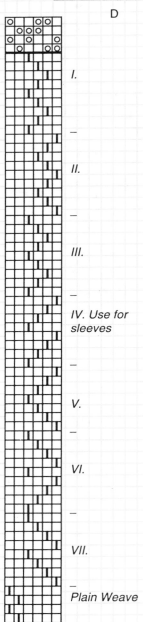

I.

—

II.

—

III.

—

IV. Use for sleeves

—

V.

—

VI.

—

VII.

—

Plain Weave

3.3. Treadling.
For body: Repeat I-VII to form desired size bands and blocks.
For sleeves: Repeat part IV for 22" in peacock and for 22" in royal.

activity. But, in fact, we most often think in two dimensions – horizontal and vertical – probably because we weave in two dimensions at the loom. We think warp, weft, horizontal, vertical, top, bottom, left and right. This spiral-seamed garment forces us *around* the body and eliminates distinctions between top and bottom, front and back. It is easy to think of a color or shape continuing from the back around to the front, or occurring just at the side of the garment. Because the vertical and horizontal weaving is re-oriented on the body, conventional bands, stripes or blocks of weaving come together in very unconventional ways, making for many creative and original designs. See Appendix 4 for several warp design possibilities based on the spiral pattern.

Some of the designs produced by my students were truly wonderful; some of the simplest were the most successful. Some versions were finished with hems and facings. Some featured knit or crochet skillfully related to the woven fabric.

After watching several classes of students develop their designs in cotton, I began to think about a unisex version in wool. My husband and two sons were after me to do something they could wear, and this seemed like a design that would work for a man.

Sampling and Weaving

My interpretation of this idea is very straightforward. I recalled a fabric I had made previously from a pattern in Davison's *A Handweaver's Pattern Book* ("Indian March," p.38) combining twill threading and treadlings to produce a patchwork look (Figs. 3.2 and 3.3) For this sweater I chose to add color changes in the blocks and add an additional pattern block.

I chose some "masculine" colors – tans, greys, and black with bright blues and purples and decided to accentuate the spiral seam with leather trim. The design relies on the offsetting of the "patchwork" blocks along the diagonal. The sleeves are woven on a separate warp threaded in one of the patchwork patterns. One of the sleeves is woven with purple weft, the other with blue. This separate warp also allowed me to make a longer sleeve than the 16-17" length determined by the width of the first warp.

3.4. Detail of diagonal pattern bands and knitted crew neck.

The sweater was finished with additional leather on the armhole seam and black ribbing at the lower edge, cuffs, and neck. I designed a crew neck for this unisex sweater. An optional woven cowl feminizes the style. Once again I chose to warp with Shetland wool and weave with both it and a 2-ply tweed. This fabric was finished much more lightly than the similar cloth for the jacket. Fig. 3.4 shows a detail of the diagonal patterning and crew neckline. Fig. 3.5 shows the warp plan for the pattern pieces. See Appendix 3 for hints on designing a neckline.

Garment Assembly

While not a loom-shaped garment, this top has relatively little sewing involved. Understanding how the pieces fit together is a bit of a 3-D puzzle, but folding the paper model (Fig. 3.1A) should aid the process. Appendix 4 contains detailed instructions for sewing this top as well as design variations.

Finishing Touches

Leather Trim. I found garment-weight leather that could be cut into stripping to my specifications at the Tandy Company in New York. I had to buy a full hide, so I decided to make a number of these sweaters for the holiday market. My *Bernina* sewing machine will easily handle garment-weight leather; some machines may not. I purchased a special needle for leather and set the stitch length at its longest. Carefully placing the leather over the seam line on the right side of the garment, I stitched

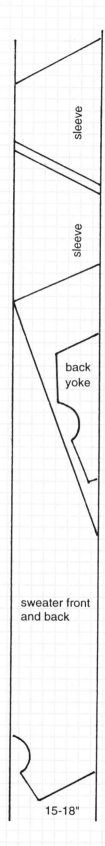

3.5. Weave Plan for Spiral Top. About 150", or 100" finished lengths plus a separate warp for sleeves 24" wide x 44" long.

3.6. Detail of leather trim across front and armhole seams.

one side, then the other. Where two ends meet, I overlapped about 1/4" and stitched across. Try to position such a join inconspicuously, under the arm, for example. A detail of the trim is shown in Fig. 3.6.

The knitted ribbing at the neck, bottom, and cuffs is 2/2 ribbing. Directions for adding ribbing to handknit fabric can be found in Appendix 8.

Comments

The shetland yarn must be fulled to match the texture of the yarn in the fabric. This can be done before knitting, but I prefer to knit first, then wash and gently rub the knit areas. Rinse and let dry.

Using this spiral-seamed top pattern will surely lead you to wonder, "Could this become a dress, a coat, a sleeve?" This is exactly the kind of thinking that makes designing and weaving clothing so addictive – one step leads to another and pretty soon you're hooked!

Un&ett-ling Isa's Sweater

MATERIALS LIST

Warp:
Silk & Wool (Tahki)
Magenta
Coral
Teal
Olive
Black

Weft:
Same
Inlay wefts
Silk
Yellow, plus various
colors for embroidery

Sett:
8 e.p.i.

Sweaters are my favorite article of clothing – particularly winter sweaters. They gratify and warm my pscyche, just like a bowl of hot soup in miserable weather. Yet as much as I enjoy wearing them, I had never woven one.

Design Process via Detour

A household weaving project that didn't work out gave me the idea. The route was circuitous, but the result was a sweater!

In between my clothing projects, I weave Scandinavian-style household articles, usually in linen. After weaving off yards of linen for window swags, I decided the windows looked better without the swags than with. Now what?!

The fabric's drapability was good for a caftan – something I could always use. Even though it meant using the dreaded sewing machine, I plowed ahead. All went well until gussets had to be fitted in under the arms. This proved to be an impossible sewing task for me. The caftan made from the swags is now pillows.

However, as I was struggling, I realized that if I had made the gussets as one long, continuous piece of fabric up the sides and under the entire sleeve, I would have the caftan instead of pillows! As the long gusset idea was forming, I could see that this idea might be applicable for a sweater. Long gussets up the sides and under the arms would allow for disjointed patterning that could make it as playful as the currently fashionable "art-knit" sweaters. Using a soft yarn with an open sett in twill weave would help to achieve a drapable fabric.

Color ideas come from everywhere. I enjoy studying the Liberty of London fabrics for the way the colors are juxtaposed and proportioned. Theatrical designers are certainly expert in color's impact. At the ballet, I watched dancers wearing persimmon, olive green, sulfur yellow, rust and pale blue - truly inspirational coloring!

Color Choices

Since this was to be a playful piece, the color choice had to set the tone. The reading I have done about color theory does not stick with me. The color "trick" I find most useful is to look for very ordinary color combinations and then alter them. In the case of red, white, and blue, instead of using a true red I would substitute a yellow red; instead of white, grey; but when choosing a blue, I would use two different blue families such as a red-blue and green-blue proportioned unequally. I have tried this with red and green, pink and blue, and all other common color combinations.

Using this system, and red, white and blue, I chose a black background (instead of white), with coral and magenta (substituted for red) and olive and teal (substituted for blue).

20"

39"

Left Gusset

Right Gusset

20 1/2"

Left Sleeve Top

Right Sleeve Top

21 1/2"

Back

21 1/2"

Front

Warp plan

Draft

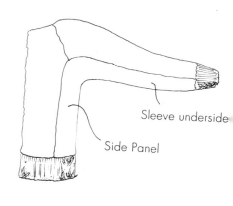

Sleeve underside

Side Panel

Gusset construction

Warp Plan and Weaving

In order to have a sweater-like drape for this garment, I found that the body and sleeves had to be full. I measured my bust to determine the warp width needed and divided that measurement in half for sweater front and back. It came to 20 inches (half or 40 inches). I made the gusset width half of the front or back panel.

For my 40-inch bust, the front and back pieces are 18 1/2 inches wide. The warp width was 20 inches. I increased the warp width by adding 10% ease plus about 10% shrinkage or draw-in. Each sleeve top and gusset is half the warp width after finishing the fabric edges with a serger.

Depending on yarn shrinkage, you might feel happier adding an extra inch to the gusset. The sweater length is whatever looks best on you.

I'll leave color theory to the experts because, for me, it would destroy its romantic and mysterious quality. You can usually describe why you like someone but when you fall in love it's impossible to tell why – it's indescribable. Well, that's the way I feel about color. It's that undefinable magic in life.

Top View of sweater

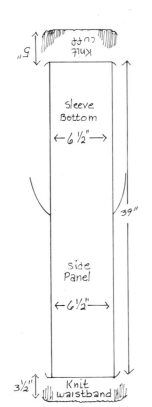

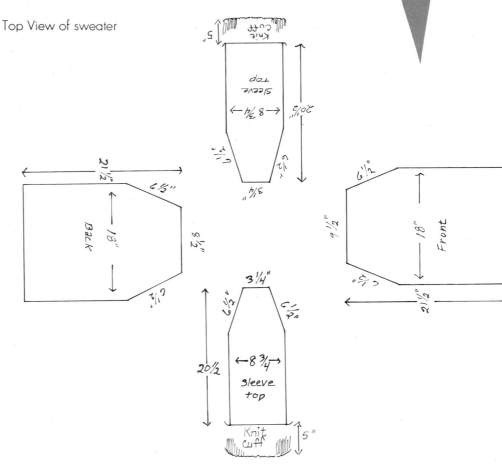

Gusset Plan

Garment Assembly Diagram

29

I wanted an asymmetrical look, so the the warp color arrangement is different on both the body and sleeves. I didn't attempt to match stripes anywhere.

I used the 2/2 twill threading for drapability, reversing its direction in the middle of the warp. I could use the twill diagonals as guides for adding yellow silk laid-in triangles – large ones on the front and smaller ones on the back. I changed the treadling to a basket weave with tabby on parts of the sleeves for solid horizontal stripes.

Garment Assembly

First I butted the seams and joined them with the baseball stitch in a finer black yarn.

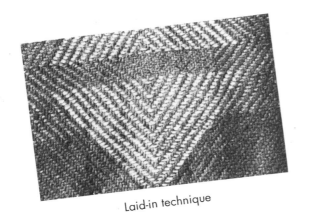

Laid-in technique

Detail, decorative stitching at shoulder seam.

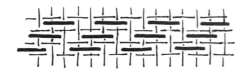

Inlay on a twill shed

Detail, gusset with decorative oversitiching.

After the seams were sewn, I added some decorative stitching. At the shoulders, I stitched the blanket stitch on each side of the seam line. Down the center of the seam line itself, I embroidered with the stem stitch. For the gusset seams, I used the the feather stitch in the olive yarn,then overlaid it with a layer of the same stitch in the magenta yarn.

Finishing Touches

For the finish, I knitted black cuffs and cowl onto the woven sweater. (See Appendix 8 for details of knitting onto woven fabric.) I added a decorative touch at the edges by trimming the cuff and bottom edges of the sweater by working a row of Backward Crochet. (See

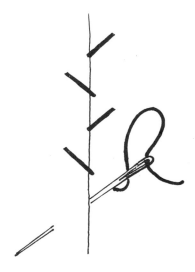

Baseball Stitch

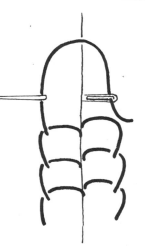

Buttonhole Stitch

Detail, sleeve with decorative seam and knitted cuff with stitched embellishments.

Appendix 7 for instructions.) In order to carry some of the sweater color into the knitted bands and collar, I added some stem-stitching at random with bits of the sweater yarns.

Comments

This sweater fits with comfortable ease. When I make this design again, I'd like to make the gussets extend beyond the bottom edge of the sweater and fold the extra length up to form pockets. The pockets could be embroidered and closed with tassels or fancy buttons.

Feather Stitch

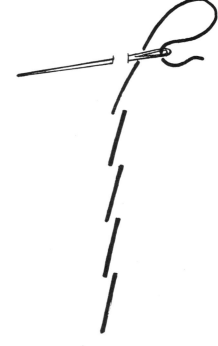

Stem Stitch

Detail, knitted cowl collar with stitched embellishments.

Design Process

A few years ago, I made a visit to my friends at a local handweaving supplier, and while there bought two skeins of incredibly beautiful, lustrous, fine silk. I usually weave at 10 to 20 ends per inch, but I knew that I should try my hand at weaving fine fabric sooner or later. I knew this would be time-consuming and would require one of my three looms to be tied up for a long time, so I needed a really good reason to begin. When Isa and I assigned ourselves an evening ensemble, that was the motivation I needed to take on the challenge.

The idea for the design came from a evening tunic of brocaded organza I saw at a party. I planned to weave irregularly shaped rectangles and triangles in a laid-in technique on a plain-weave ground. These shapes would be grouped more or less densely, creating a design element which would flow gracefully from neck and shoulders to hem. The first sketch (Fig. 4.1) was satisfactory as a working drawing (probably because I had been thinking of this design for some time before I sat down with my pencil and paper).

Sampling

The first step was to work out the colors. One of the silk skeins was a lavender reeled silk; the other was a mint green Doupionni with a small slub. Since I wanted to use them both, the reeled silk in the warp and the slubbed in the weft, I decided to over-dye the mint green skein. It became a bluish lilac shade that worked well with the reddish lavender warp. I ordered several shades of silks in jewel tones, and selected several metallics from my shelves to use for the inlaid shapes. The next step was to determine sett. (See Appendix 1 for sett and shrinkage information.)

I had no extra silk to squander as a sample, since each skein, although the yardage looked infinite, was actually only about 4 ounces. My sample, therefore, was very small – about 2" wide, but it did show me that 45 ends per inch would be acceptable, though the sett could have been much closer. The resulting fabric is taffeta-like, with a slight texture from the slubby weft. I decided that, since I was weaving plain weave, if I had enough silk for the warp, the chances were good that I would also have enough for the weft, as the skeins were of equal weight and the silks appeared to be of similar thickness. Figures 4.2 and 4.3 give the threading and treadling.

Warping

To prepare the warp, I put my skein on the swift and wound a ball using approximately half the skein. I wound two threads at a time, one from the ball and one from the swift, onto my warping board. (Throughout this project, I wished that I had gotten my hands into a hand lotion regime before beginning!) The silk caught easily and snagged on everything. Usually the thread didn't break, but when this did occur, the filaments

Materials

Top:
Warp::
Fine reeled silk *(mill ends)*
lavender

Weft:
Fine douppioni silk *(mill ends)*
lilac

Inlay wefts:
Medium-weight silk *(Halcyon Gemstone)*
Assorted metallic yarns

Sett:
45 e.p.i.

Skirt:
Warp:
Plied silk *(mill ends)*

Weft:
Medium-weight silk *(Halcyon Gemstone)*
Assorted metallic yarns

Sett:
8 e.p.i.

4.1 Evening ensemble.

4.5. Evening ensemble. Silk top with inlay and plain weave skirt in metallic yarns.

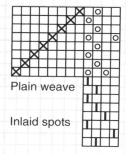

Plain weave

Inlaid spots

4.2. Draft for top.

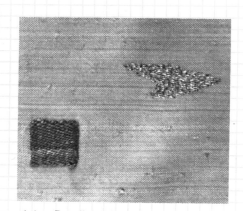

4.4.a. Detail, inlaid motifs, actual size.

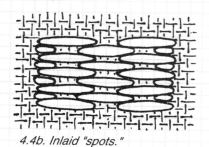

4.4b. Inlaid "spots."

were pulled apart and weakened. I transferred the warp from board to loom in small sections, threading it in a straight draw on my 8-harness loom. It seemed prudent to thread the heddles first, then wind on and dent the reed last. The twill threading made it possible to treadle a tie down for the brocade every 8 threads, making the weft floats between 1/5" and 1/6", short enough not to catch. I alternated tie-downs between harnesses 4 and 8. (Figs. 4.4 a and b and 4.5.)

Threading with material this fine was a new experience for me, and this particular silk was exasperating, requiring all the patience I could muster. It was not heavy enough for gravity to affect it as I threaded – it sometimes floated right back out of the heddles. It had an affinity to anything proximate, whether the adjacent threads or my slightly rough hands. Dampening the threads as I worked seemed to help. I consulted Cheryl Kolander's fine book *A Silk Worker's Notebook,* for assistance and found this statement: "Weaving with silk is truly the subject to fill another book." (p. 137). I concur.

Beaming the warp was the hardest job. It was slow work getting the warp's threads to separate and slide smoothly through the heddles. My "smooth" lease sticks had to be sanded with steel wool. Threads broke in the process, and I decided to use an overhand knot to reconnect them because the thread was extremely slippery. After the warp was wound on the back beam, I removed the lease sticks, inserted a 15-dent reed and sleyed it at 3 threads per dent. This warp proved that it's best to be flexible about methods for dressing the loom, depending on the material you are dealing with. Fig. 4.7 shows the weave plan for the pattern pieces.

4.6. Detail, bands of metallic threads on left sleeve.

Weaving Layout:

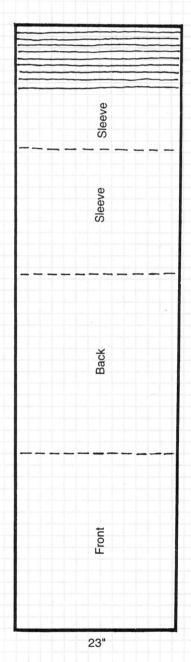

Weaving

Once I began weaving, I had very few broken threads – a good thing, as my patience was already exhausted! Some of my usual weaving practices failed me on this warp: I replaced one broken warp, weighted it with a washer, pinned it to the fell, wove 8 to 10 inches and removed the pin as I usually do. The silk was so slippery that the weight of the washer in the back was enough to pull the new thread completely out! For the next broken warp, I didn't try to remove the pin.

My sketch didn't indicate the exact placement of any of the inlaid shapes – I "composed" at the loom, following the general plan on the drawing (Fig. 4.1). I did have to consider the finished shape of the pattern pieces I would be using, so that the design would fall with the seam lines.

A Detour!

As I neared the end of the weaving, which as anticipated did take an enormous amount of time, it became clear that my optimism about the amount of weft I possessed was wishful thinking. Isa sympathized. I began to consider my options. I was also beginning to think about weaving fabric for a skirt, so the shortage of silk weft didn't seem like a disaster, but a chance instead to coordinate the two pieces more closely. I decided to weave narrow weft-faced stripes for the lower portion of the left sleeve (Fig. 4.6). On a new warp, (a plied silk sett at 8 e.p.i.), I wove wide weft-faced stripes for a short skirt. The colors were those already used for the brocaded shapes.

4.7. Weave plan for top.

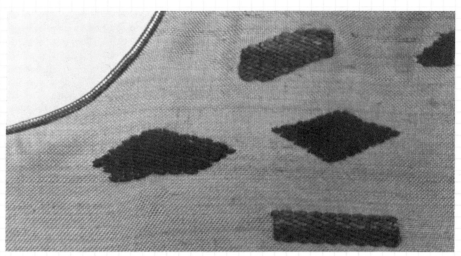

4.8. Detail, metallic piping at neckline.

Fabric Finishing

To finish the fabric, I washed the silk by hand in warm water and hung it to dry without wringing it, then pressed it on the wrong side. There is a slight crispness to the finished fabric.

Garment Assembly

I decided to line the top with organza to add to the crisp appearance of the silk. I stitched the organza and silk pieces together and treated them as one. I used a metallic cording which matched the copper-colored metallic of the top to emphasize the neckline edge and the hems of the sleeves (Figs. 4.8 and 4.9). A covered button corded loop completed the neck opening. The skirt was interlined for stability with a lightweight fusible iron-on interfacing and lined with a polyester lining fabric. (See Appendix 2 for information on working with linings, interlinings, facings, and interfacings.)

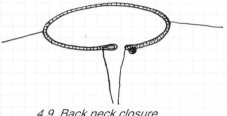

4.9. Back neck closure.

Comments

I often think beginning weavers have a big advantage over experienced ones; once we know how much work and time is involved in a project, it may become a factor in our design decisions. Many of my successful early pieces were very complex technically, using double-weave pick-up, tapestry inlay, or a combination of the two. These were definitely one-of-a-kind works.

That is how I presently feel about this silk brocade piece. It will be a while before I tackle this technique and material again, but I do intend to continue to explore weaving with fine thread. With fine threads, a pattern is naturally miniaturized, and I prefer large-scale patterns that can become an integral part of a garment design. The challenge for me is to find ways to avoid making cloth that looks commercially woven, but instead has a graphic element that could only be handwoven.

MATERIALS

Jacket Warp:
2-ply Wool
Blue

Weft:
Heavy silk singles
Green
Grape
Grey
Blue

Sett:
8 e.p.i.

Dress Warp and Weft:
2-ply Silk (The Silk Tree)

Sett:
24 e.p.i.

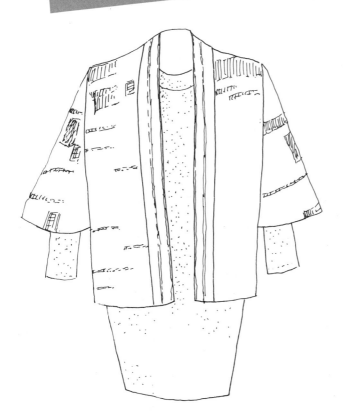

Our son was getting married – a wonderful opportunity for a great celebration and a great dress. The bride's family was responsible for the wedding and all I had to do was to worry about what I'd wear. How tempted I was to buy a dress; but this was a coward's way out. I knew I had to weave it. But for me to face this project meant no detours, errors, or redos, since time was of the essence. This was a daunting thought for me as I had never gone straight to "go." There could be none of my usual now what!? I had to weave my dress for another reason as well; my son, Andy, has made my weaving life so much easier – at first by helping me to beam my warp, and later by making, improving, and sometimes inventing new equipment for me.

Design Process

When I decided to make my outfit, I took stock of my physical assets and deficits as well as my yarn supply. It was an afternoon wedding in early November, so a short dress and jacket seemed just right. My legs are still good, albeit a little blue, and my upper arms are beginning to flag. Also, I am highwaisted. Translation: a top-of-the-knee length dress with long sleeves and no waist – chemise style. This style should accentuate the positives and camouflage the negatives. As for the jacket, I think the kimono style is a flattering form as well as being a traditional woven garment. Mine would have a woven band to trim the front edges.

Silk was the appropriate fiber, and I had recently bought some thick, lustrous silk with a minimal twist at a friend's yarn sale. I had about a pound at 700 yards per pound. The colors were in uneven quantities of silver-toned blue, green, grape and grey.

As a rule I try never to buy more yarn to augment a project in the works. This becomes an aid to me in designing. Too many choices create chaos. Yarn limitations help to organize my ideas and force solutions that I might never have thought of.

The simplest part was the dress. I had pounds of fine slubbed grey silk which would be woven as yardage in a 3-1 twill. I would use *Simplicity* pattern #9311 for sewing the dress.

Designing the kimono was problematical, as I had not enough of the heavier silk to sample with. I thought that satin weave would showcase the yarns, but the fabric would be too heavy.

It has often been said that timing is everything in life. I attended a guild meeting program that month on "Shaft-Switching Made Easy." The idea was to weave patterned rugs with the shaft-switching aided by the use of jewelry clasps. Why not try this technique for clothing? And why not for the kimono?

The shaft-switching technique allows the weaver to have many more color blocks than would normally be available on a 4-harness loom, or for that matter, depending on the amount of switching, on an 8-harness loom. It is accomplished by having one thread lie between two heddles that are on adjacent harnesses. The warp can be attached with a jewelry clasp to either

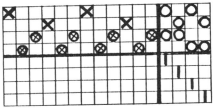

Shaft Switching

Jacket Draft

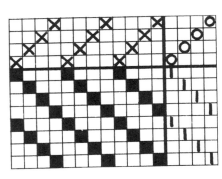

1/3 Twill

Dress Draft

Detail of fabric with shaft-switching used to alter blocks of color (medium and dark areas). The light area is achieved by using two shuttles in a "meet-and-separate" weaving technique.

heddle on any pick. The limited amounts of silk I had could be utilized effectively with this technique.

Shaft switching is done as a two-color weft-faced weave. I began weaving with two shuttles wound with blue and green. To add more color interest, I wove some areas with additional wefts in a "meet-and-separate" weave. See Appendix 7 for shaft-switching and pattern details.

A Plan!!

A carefully organized blueprint for the kimono design was a necessity in order to distribute the colors over the garment and still have enough silk remaining to do the finishing band. For me this was a new thought process. I drew a geometric design on graph paper. The geometric hard edge made an interesting contrast with the silk's softness. The warp had to be textured to grab the silk, yet strong and pliable enough for clothing. It also had to be set at 8 epi, because a closer sett would make shaft switching impossibly tedious. I chose a 2-ply blue wool. Its texture could hold the silk so it would not pack down.

Weaving

As the weaving progressed and I was carefully following the drawing, my mind felt as though it were in a vise. I was obsessed with following my drawing and there was definitely no room for my usual detours. But true to form, problems began to arise – my weaving salvation.

Inevitable Detours

The color plan that I had drawn was not working; I didn't have enough of the colors I had selected for the design. I reorganized them and set aside enough for the warp-faced band that I planned for the kimono trim. By weaving the front and back pieces first, I used the colors I had the most of, simplifying the design to use fewer colors. The sleeves, woven last, had more shaft switches and more complex coloring because I knew by then how much of each color I had remaining. Instead of the

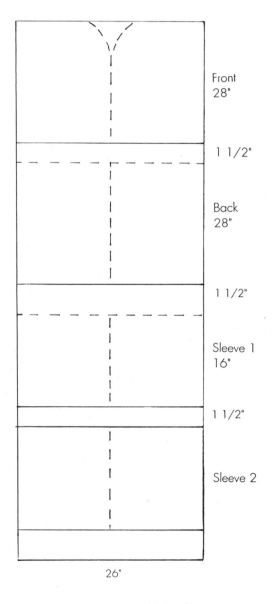

Front
28"

1 1/2"

Back
28"

1 1/2"

Sleeve 1
16"

1 1/2"

Sleeve 2

26"

Warp plan

body having the main interest, it was now on the sleeves.

A major problem arose with the jewelry clasps which frayed the warp, causing it to break frequently. That method is good for rug warp sett at 4 epi, but the wool warp was too fine and the 8 epi sett was just too close! Besides, opening and closing the clasps hurt my fingers. There had to be an easier way that would be quick and inexpensive. Garbage bag tie-ups proved to be the answer! I cut them into half-inch lengths; they held the warp easily by making one twist and pressing the twist against the heddle shaft.

Garment Assembly

The kimono construction was quite easy, consisting of all straight seams. I made a v-shaped neck which allows the warp-faced band to lie flat. One sewing trick I learned along the way was to make a slanted seam at the shoulder. For some reason the slant allows a jacket to hang well without any dips at the hem. I folded the sleeves in half and set them in.

Finishing Touches

When I removed the kimono from the loom, I could see that the revamped design was more interesting now with the highlights on the sleeves. It could be more interesting with a bit of added texture to enhance the flat surface, so I embroidered stem stitches at random. (See page 36.)

I wove a striped warp-faced edging band twice the desired trim width and machine-stitched it onto the right side of the jacket. I turned the band to the inside and tacked it down. When the lining was put in, it covered the edge of the band.

Before I began this project, I took a 12-inch strand of the silk and washed it. This bit of sampling proved very valuable because the silk lost its lustre and I decided not to wash the fabric. When it came time to press the kimono, I used a pressing cloth and ironed it on the wrong side with a steam iron, which slightly fulled the wool warp and improved the drape of the fabric.

I had the kimono lined with silk to facilitate putting it on. The dress's fit was greatly improved with large shoulder pads, so I did not need them in the kimono.

Comments

It was a special feeling for me to wear this outfit and it proved to be worth all the effort. The plain grey silk twill chemise was the perfect foil for the kimono. I even enjoyed figuring out a way to get what I wanted through loom control.

Woven band trim.
Note stem stitch detail in white
on jacket.

Cascading Wrap

Pat: One day when we were meeting to work on the rewrites for this book, Isa arrived and announced that she had been window shopping in New York and had seen an exciting jacket style. She even brought along a rudimentary pattern which she and another weaving friend had worked out.

Materials

Warp and weft:
2-ply alpaca *(On The Inca Trail)*

Sett:
10 e.p.i.
very little shrinkage (1-2%)

Isa: Poking around offbeat shops is a good source for ideas. I get to see unusual shapes, color combinations, closures – whatever is avant garde – which are often adaptable to weaving. I had long wanted to weave a jacket with cascading lapels. Pat and I discovered that we had each been working on this idea. I had made many attempts, but they were never what I was hoping for. One of these tries, a coat, was fairly successful. Hoping to achieve a cascading front, I made the front pieces wider than the back. My thought was that the extra width would drape. When I tried on the coat, it was obvious that this was not quite the solution. Once again the Detour! In order to have enough fabric for sleeves, I had to cut the coat hem to jacket length. I then used that material for the full sleeves originally planned. The end result is a jacket with an asymmetrical closing. I made the front edges irregular by cutting out small rectangles and trimming it with a bias band knit in a highly contrasting color.

In New York I spotted the style that I had been seeking in a commercially made taffeta coat. I felt as though I had found the unicorn or the pot of gold . . . this was it! With the help of a cooperative saleswoman and my friend, we were able to understand the cutting trick that made it work. An intriguing aspect of the cut is that it is symmetrical when worn open and is asymmetrical when closed.

E.1. Alpaca Jacket/Wrap designed by Pat and Isa for limited production.

Pat: I can always rely on Isa's eye for style and color, but for her to think about a pattern was a new departure. When she showed it to me my internal computer went into action and I went immediately to my pile of uncompleted projects and found the very shape – except that I had not figured out the way to cut it. This was one of those projects started in a dry period; when all else fails, just get *something* on the loom was my operating mode at the time. My inspiration had come from a photo of an Issey Miyake knit coat. Once the trick was revealed – and it was so easy – all I could say was, "Why didn't I think of that!" It doesn't take too many of these humbling episodes to realize that there is nothing new under the sun in weaving, or probably anywhere else. Some ancient people probably have done it first and better.

I don't think creativity is precluded under these circumstances if something new and personal is introduced. I think of the kimono shape as a canvas and I think of this jacket/wrap as a canvas, also. Once the *aha!* struck, our pattern evolved through a number of stages, each involving some refinements over the previous version. From a two-piece pattern (sleeves excluded) with a center back seam, it became a three-piece pattern with side seams into which pockets were inserted. Skimpy sleeves, which were a remainder of the original pattern pieces, became a generous full length. There was severe stress at the point of the armhole slit, so a small dart was taken which eliminated the problem (Fig. E.1).

Collaboration

As we were working out the kinks, we began to consider the idea of collaborating to produce a line of these jackets. We developed several design ideas that we thought were really good. It seemed like our opposite approaches might actually result in a wearable, saleable garment. We would each do our own designs. I would do the sewing and Isa would do the promotion. See Figs. E.2A and B.

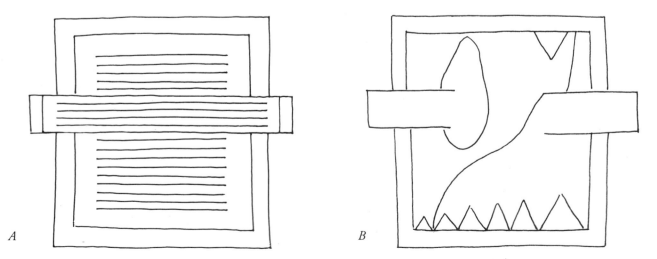

A   *B*

E.2A and B. Jacket/wrap designs.
Warp length: 206" plus loom waste. Woven in plain weave with stripes, bands, inlays according to your design.

Isa: Some of the aspects of this joint venture struck terror in my heart. We had chosen a luxe fiber, alpaca, and I didn't want any more detours. The first design I made required precision weaving, as there were inlays that had to match up along the seams. Symmetry is either good design and discipline, or it is a trap. This time I had to believe in the former. I measured constantly! When the fabric was cut off the loom for delivery to Pat to sew, I quite frankly lacked the courage to see if it did match. I still wonder what I would have done if it hadn't.

As we received more orders for this jacket, I found that, within the confines of its shape, I can do my usual ad lib at the loom. As the shape is predetermined, designing within its form is very challenging. Pat enjoys using tapestry techniques and I prefer selvage-to-selvage ones. This led me to think of using borders in an unusual way, some meet-and-separate weave, and some laid-in.

Pat and Isa: We have found collaborating a useful and very productive way of accomplishing disparate tasks. We think it worked for us because of our mutual appreciation of each other's abilities and viewpoints. We highly recommend it.

Step-by-step assembly instructions for this jacket/wrap follow.

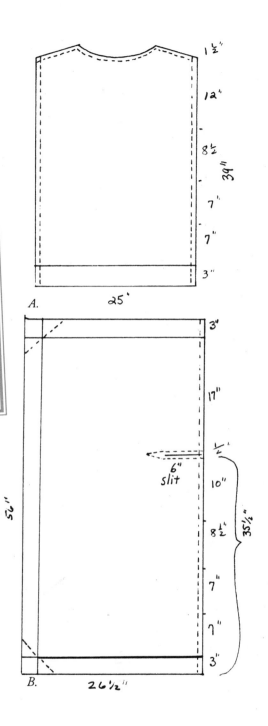

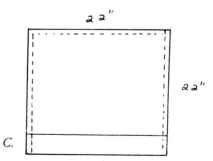

E.3. Garment warp and cutting plan. A. Front. B. Back. C. Collar.

43

Fabric Finishing

Machine wash the fabric in luke-warm water on the gentle cycle for two to three minutes of agitation. Rinse, and spin dry. Press while still damp, then roll the fabric around a tube and let it dry. As the exterior layer dries, peel it from the roll.

This method helps counteract the 'tracking' which tends to occur with this yarn.

Give the dry fabric a final steam pressing.

Lining

Prepare lining pieces first as shown at right.

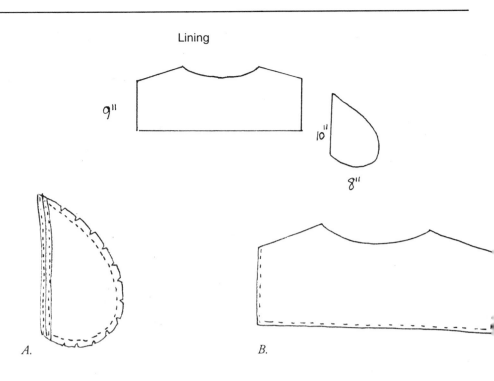

Lining

9"

10"

8"

A.

B.

E.4. Lining pieces.
A. Pocket has a 1/8" hem. Turn under 1/8", stitch, turn under 1/8" again and stitch. Sew right sides together with 1/4" seam. Clip seam allowance. Turn pocket inside out and press.

B. Make 1/8" hem on back facing side and bottom edges.

E4. Another way to wear this wrap. The jacket can be made somewhat longer, but take care that the cascading front does not near the floor.

Garment Assembly
Body

1. Reinforce slits on garment front. (See Fig. E.6A.

2. Cut slits.

3. Join collar/hood back seam with a French seam (Fig. E.6B).

    A. Sew wrong sides together 1/8" to 1/4" from edge.

    B. Turn. Right sides are now together. Press seam flat.

    C. Stitch 3/8" from enclosed edge.

    D. Press flat. Topstitch.

4. Join back to fronts (Fig. E.7A).

    A. Pin right sides together matching points C, B, and A.

    B. Stitch a 5/8" seam. First, stitch from B to C to B. Backstitch at beginning and end of stitching. Then stitch from A to B. Backstitch. This will create a small fold of extra fabric at B on the front piece. Sew a dart about 3 - 3 1/2" long at point B. (See Fig. E.7B.)

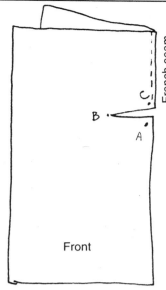

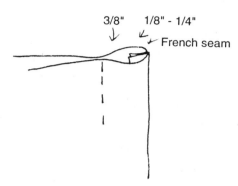

E.6A. Garment front with slit.

E.6B. French seam.

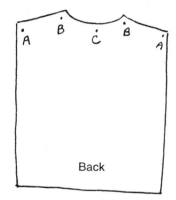

E.7A. Back. Dots indicate points to match on front and back when joining to collar and facing.

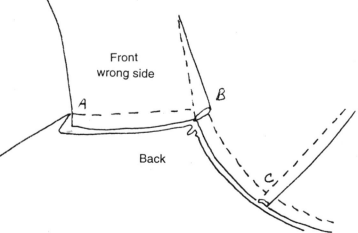

E.7B. Collar/shoulder seam. A dart is formed at point B.

Facing

1. Attach back facing following Figs. E.8A and B.

   A. Stitch from point *A* to point *B*. Backstitch.

   B. Stitch from point *B* to point *C*, to point *B* on the other side. Backstitch.

2. Turn facing and press, clipping and trimming seam allowance as necessary.

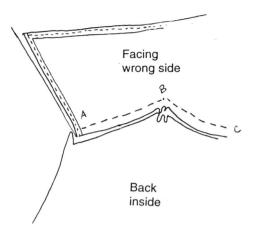

Facing
wrong side

B

A

C

Back
inside

E.8A. Facing attached to back piece first.

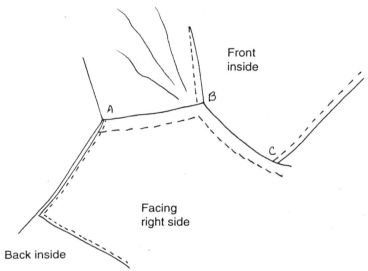

Front
inside

A

B

C

Back inside

Facing
right side

3. Topstitch facing 3/8" from seam, as in fig. E8B.

E.8B. Facing attached to front and topstitched.

Side seam and Pockets

1. Stitch a 1" side seam, using twill tape or seam binding as shown to reinforce the areas above and below pocket inset, Fig. E.9A. Backstitch at beginning and end of stitching.

2. Stitch pocket to right side of seam allowance, Fig. E.9B. See page 22 for details of attaching a pocket into a seam allowance.

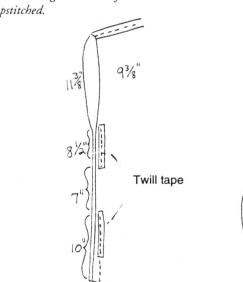

$11\frac{3}{8}"$
$9\frac{3}{8}"$

$8\frac{1}{2}"$

Twill tape

$7"$

$10"$

E.9A. Twill tape or seam binding added for reinforcement.

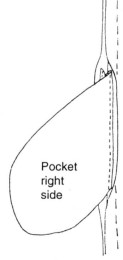

Pocket
right
side

E.9B. Pocket attached to seam allowance.

Hem

Press hem under 1/2" and again 2 1/2". Miter hem at inside corners, as in Fig. E.10A. Trim off excess at corner to 1/2". Press corner seam open. Turn, press, hem (Fig. E.10B).

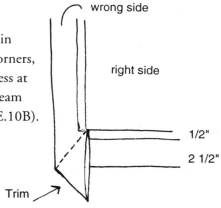
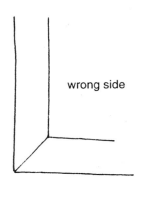

wrong side

right side

wrong side

1/2"

2 1/2"

Trim

E.10A. Mitered corner of hem.

E.10B. Completed hem.

Sleeves

Seam the underarm seam with a French seam.

A. Press sleeve hem under 1/2" and again 2 1/2". Finish remaining edge by serging or other means.

B. Insert sleeve, matching center of sleeve to shoulder line as shown in Fig. E.11.

11. Complete sleeve hems.

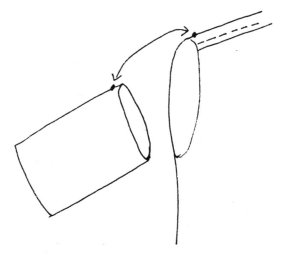

E.11. Attaching sleeve.

Closure

Use a large covered hook and eye and a fabric-covered snap, if desired, to close the jacket. Attach on inside where indicated by X. (Fig. E.12.)

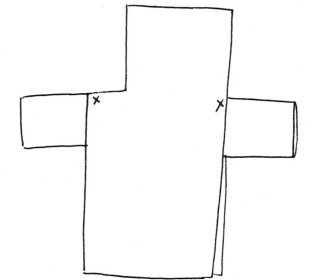

E.12. Adding fasteners.

Determining Shrinkage

A question that is often asked has to do with how to take shrinkage into account when weaving clothing. This matter is complicated by the factors of take-up required for the interlacement of the weave structure, and also by draw-in, the decrease in width resulting from both take-up and weft tension. To compensate for all of this, if the fabric is an all-over pattern, simply weave enough extra fabric to allow for the percentage of shrinkage shown in your sample.

However, if you are "engineering" a design into your cloth that is meant to appear at a predetermined place or places on the garment, you can:

1. Draw a cartoon that is larger by the appropriate percentage than the finished pattern piece; pin it underneath the warp as you are weaving and use it as a guide.

2. Establish an interval of measurement and add the amount of shrinkage into that. For example, for every 12" of finished weaving, weave 13 1/2" and enlarge the design elements in that 13 1/2" accordingly (from the desired size in the finished 12"). This method works well with the spiral-seamed top because the side line and center front and back lines are good "markers." Weave what you have designed proportionately larger, between the predetermined interval.

3. Loom-shaped garments (or partially loom-shaped) require a similar strategy. All the critical finished measurements (armhole depth, neck opening, width, length, etc.) must be increased in the weaving by the appropriate percentage.

Whenever possible, I try to leave myself a margin for error. For example, several extra inches between pattern pieces will allow for shifting the placement for cutting, if necessary. All the pre-planning in the world won't eliminate some surprises, and a safety net is always a good idea.

A.1A. Woven fabric as taken from the loom. Note elongated design blocks.

A.1B. Fulled fabric after washing.

Lazy Sampling

If you feel quite certain about a warp's sett – whether from experience or manufacturer's, or supplier's suggestions – you can add about 1/2 yard when you wind your warp and do what we call lazy sampling. Try several possible techniques, yarns, colors, etc. on the first 12 inches. Cut off and retie the warp (or use the quicker technique shown in Figure A.1). Stitch with a serger or use a running zigzag stitch to prevent the edges of the sample from raveling.

Measure the sample and record the measurement. Finish the fabric by washing and drying it. Remeasure and calculate the shrinkage. If you wish to try two different finishing methods, cut the sample in half lengthwise; measure in both warp and weft directions before and after. For example, you might want to agitate one sample more than the other and compare the drape or the variable shrinkage of ground and pattern yarns.

To check on color fastness or shrinkage, wash 10" lengths of the yarns in question in hot water. Let them dry on a white paper towel. Check to see if any color has bled onto the paper. Remeasure the lengths of yarn. Using a 10" length makes estimating the percentage of shrinkage easy. A 9 1/2" length means there has been 5% shrinkage. This "laziness" is recommended only in limited circumstances. You must know exactly the amount of shrinkage in the warp to be able to place your designs accurately in any project.

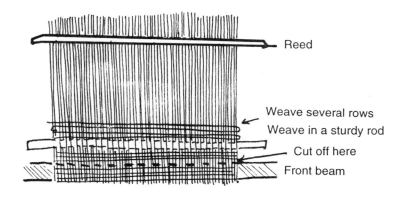

Reed

Weave several rows
Weave in a sturdy rod

Cut off here
Front beam

A.1. Quick technique for cutting off a sample and retying the warp.
1. After the sample is finished, weave a heading, weave in a rod, then weave several more rows to secure it. Cut off the sample.
2. Lash the woven-in rod to warp beam. Weave several rows of a new heading.

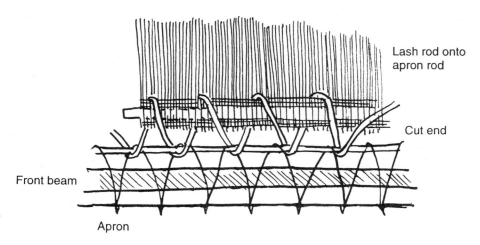

Lash rod onto apron rod

Cut end

Front beam

Apron

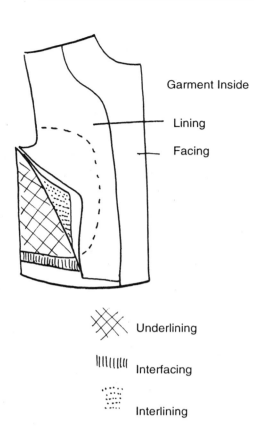

Garment Inside

Lining

Facing

⨯⨯⨯ Underlining

‖‖‖‖ Interfacing

⠂⠂⠂ Interlining

A.2A. Lining layers.

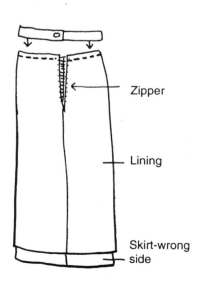

Zipper

Lining

Skirt-wrong side

A.2B. Skirt lining.

If linings, facings, interlinings, interfacings and underlinings are a mystery to you, you are overlooking some important ways to assure that your garments do not look homemade. Lining layers are shown in Fig. A.2A.

Definitions

Lining – A lightweight, usually smooth, often slippery inner shell for a garment. It covers the seams and other construction, provides some body, and allows the garment to slide on easily.

Facings – Shaped edges for necklines, jacket fronts, etc., usually cut from the same fabric as the garment. Either folded back and pressed – a hem can be thought of as a facing – or stitched right sides together along the seam line, turned and pressed to finish raw edges of a garment.

Interfacing – a variety of specially designed fabrics, varying in firmness, used in small areas, such as collars, necklines, hems, and jacket and coat front edges, to add shape, stability, and firmness to the garment.

Interlinings – An extra lining between the lining and underlining or garment added for warmth.

Underlining – A layer of lining fabric cut the same size as the garment pattern pieces, stitched to the garment fabric, and treated as one in further garment construction.

Some ways to use these layers in handwoven clothing

Linings

These can be indispensable, giving handwovens a quality look. A lining (and an underlining) can prevent the back of a skirt from "sitting out," reduce wrinkling, protect your skin from any scratchy fibers and help preserve the shape of the garment.

To cut a lining for a skirt, you can usually use the garment pattern pieces and assemble them as you did the outer garment. Before adding the waistband, baste the lining and garment together at the waist seam, wrong sides together. Fold lining seam allowances on zipper opening to inside and blind stitch to the zipper (Fig. A.2B). Attach waistband. Hem the skirt and its lining separately.

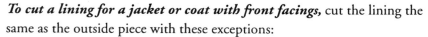

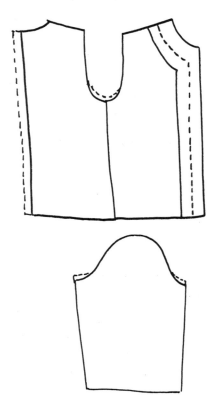

A.2C. Jacket lining pieces. Cut from garment pattern pieces with the following alterations:
1. Add 1" pleat to center back.
2. Add 1/4" to underarm on body and sleeve.
3. Cut away the area that overlaps the facing, leaving a seam allowance.
4. Cut length to finished edge of outer garment.

To cut a lining for a jacket or coat with front facings, cut the lining the same as the outside piece with these exceptions:

1. Add a 1" pleat at the center back, either just at the neckline, tapering to nothing at the hem, or the entire length of the center back line of the jacket or coat (Fig. A.2C).

2. Cut away the areas of the lining that overlap with facings, but leave a seam allowance so that the lining can be seamed to the facing edges.

3. Cut the underarm and armhole about 1/4" higher at the underarm seam.

4. Cut the lining so that when hemmed the length will be 1/4" to 3/4" shorter than the garment.

To insert a coat or jacket lining:

1. The complete lining is sewn together including sleeves. Then the lining and the facing are sewn, right sides together from the front hem edge up around the back neck down to the other hem edge. The armhole seams are then tacked together to hold the sleeve lining in place, or:

2. Sew lining fronts and back together at side seams and shoulder seams. Turn under 5/8" on lining front edges and back neck edge, and press. To do this neatly, sew a line of machine stitching along the 5/8" seam line. Where there is a curve, clip from the outside edge just to the stitched line in enough places so the 5/8" seam can be turned under smoothly. Pin lining into the garment. Hand-stitch in place. Baste the armhole seams of the lining and garment together. Turn sleeve armhole seams under 5/8", press, and blind-stitch to the garment and lining armhole. When hemming a lining of this type to the garment, allow a pleat at the bottom to allow for movement of the lining without stress (Fig. A.2D).

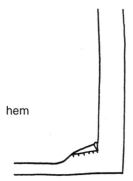

hem

A.2D. Hem the lining so a small pleat is formed, providing ease of movement.

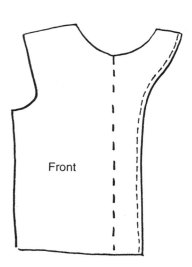

A2E 1. Cut facing as one with bodice front.

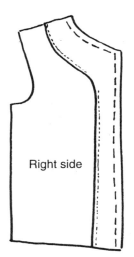

A2E 2. Separate facing. Stitch 5/8" seam, then trim, turn so wrong sides are together, and press.

Facings

Handweavers often avoid cutting facings – probably to avoid having to weave extra fabric – and try instead to finish necklines and other edges by turning under or enclosing with bias tape. These are generally unsatisfactory solutions; these methods often curl and refuse to lie flat. Cut facings asnd interfacings by using the pattern as a guide. (Figs. A.2E1-4). They should be wide enough to be invisible and unobtrusive when turned and sewn in place. If there is no extra handwoven fabric for facings, it is possible to use a harmonious commercial fabric.

An advantage to using a generously cut facing is that it provides some stability and can also cover a layer of needed interfacing.

Another advantage to using a facing is that understitching can be used to get a crisp, flat edge that may otherwise be difficult to achieve with a lofty or thick handwoven fabric.

Interfacings

Specially designed interfacing fabrics come in two forms – fusible and non-fusible. Choice of the right interfacing to give shape and stability is critical if it is to do its job. The only way to get the right results is to keep a variety of these fabrics on hand and to test before using.

The fusible interfacings may not fuse properly to fuzzy handwovens. A test sample will give you the information you need. Sometimes the pressing needed to fuse the interfacing may crush the handwoven, changing its character. Fusibles, when chosen and applied properly can add much to the appearance and performance of handwoven fabric. Lightweight fusibles can also be used on the large pattern pieces as underlining.

Non-fusible or stitch-in interfacings can be basted onto pattern pieces and caught into seams or caught to the fabric with invisible hand stitching.

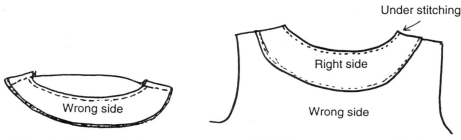

A2E3. Stitch facing to bodice front, right sides together.

A2E4. Trim seam, turn, press. Understitch close to edge, by stitching through facing and seam allowances only.

Hems

One of the best uses of interfacing in handwoven clothing is to make an invisible hem. Often the hem shows on an otherwise professional looking handwoven garment. This is usually caused not by the stitches themselves showing, but the weight of the hem hanging from those stitches, which creates a ridge or a shadow.

To prevent this, use a bias strip of interfacing about 1" wider than the hem will be. Position the strip so that it is 1/2" below finished hem line and catch-stitch it to the garment on both edges. If the interfacing is fusible, simply fuse it instead of catch-stitching. Turn the hem up and press only near the fold, not at top edge, to prevent a line. The raw edge of the hem should be given a very flat finish, such as a running zigzag, or line of straight stitching. Then, catch-stitch the raw edge of the hem to the interfacing only, not through to the garment fabric underneath (Fig. A.2F).

This technique can be used at the hem of a sleeve, too. If the fabric is very heavy, I use what I call "support stitching" in the hem. This can sometimes help a hem even if done without the interfacing. In this technique, I blind-stitch the hem to the garment interfacing about halfway up the hem and also at the raw edge of the hem. This is like two hemmings and reduces the weight on the top line of hemming.

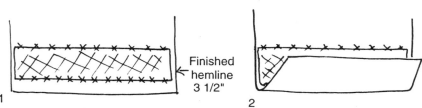

A.2F. Interfaced hem.
1. Catch-stitch bias strip of interfacing at top and bottom.
2. Fold hem up and press only at hemline.
3. Catch-stitch hem edge to interfacing.

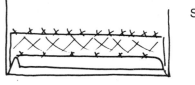

Support stitching

An additional line of hemming can add support to heavier fabrics.

Catch-stitch, or Herringbone stitch for elasticity in hemming.

The smallest possible neckline would just encircle a person's neck, which is 4-5" front to back and 6-7" side to side (Fig. A.3A). It is obvious that a round hole will not do. To further complicate matters, the natural shoulder line is not at the middle of the neck (front to back) but about 2/3 of the way toward the back. The smallest neck hole that would lie flat would require an additional opening to get it over the head and would look like a keyhole; the size of a typical head is 21-23" in circumference, so the smallest size opening that will fit comfortably would theoretically be about a 12" slit – not allowing much for a hairdo. This 12" slit will wrinkle front and back because it doesn't take the shape of the neck into consideration

A rectangle will compensate: 11 x 1" or 10 x 2" are the minimum sizes, but the wrinkle will still occur. It begins to disappear when the depth is increased to 3 1/2" or 4". The width can be reduced to about 8". These rectangular openings will fit better if 2/3 of the opening is toward the front and 1/3 to the back. (Fig. A.3B). This results in a garment in which the distance from the shoulder to the hem in the back is somewhat longer than from the shoulder to the front hem.

The neckline can also have curved lines. Some possible opening shapes are pictured in Fig. A.3C.

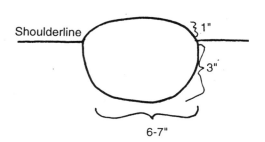

A.3A. Neckline placement.

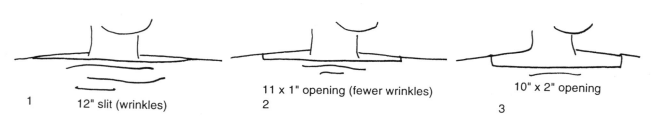

1   12" slit (wrinkles)   11 x 1" opening (fewer wrinkles)   10" x 2" opening
    2   3

A.3B. Neckline slit options: 1. 12-inch slit. 2. 11 x 1" slit. 3. 10" x 2" slit.

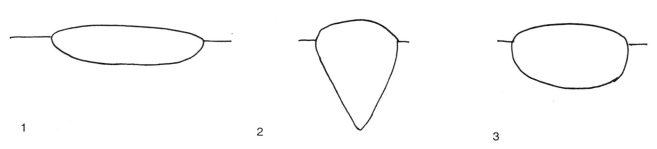

1   2   3

A.3C. Neckline shapes. 1. Oval. 2. V-neck. 3. Round neck.

You can choose to try one or more of the following:

1. Make several copies of the paper model. Sketch ideas for bands, stripes, blocks, or motifs. Fold as shown and refine the design. Or, fold the model first and then position the bands, stripes, blocks, or motifs. Notice in the illustration that the placement of the top back must be considered. Sleeves are also part of the total design (Fig. A.4A). (Remember, the back and front can be switched. See page 59.)

2. Explore the huge number of possibilities for adding the design elements decided upon in #1. On a plain weave, one-color warp, some of these include selvage-to-selvage stripes or bands of color or texture, meet-and-separate and other tapestry techniques to create blocks or other shapes, inlay, brocading, or supplementary warp patterning.

If you begin to think about weaves other than plain weave and the addition of color and/or texture in the warp, the possibilities are endless (Fig. A.4B).

3. Warp your loom and weave and sew your idea into being. To be certain of the amount of shrinkage that will occur in the warp, try the techniques of "lazy sampling" outlined in Appendix 1. For this project, I recommend that your design not depend on absolutely exact matching – leave some room for error in your design plan.

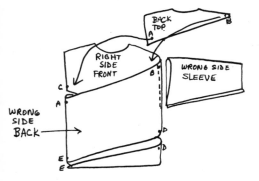

A.4A. Schematic diagram for Spiral Sweater.

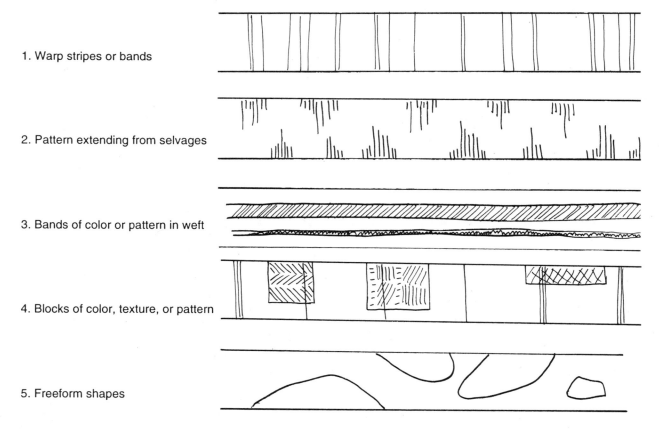

1. Warp stripes or bands

2. Pattern extending from selvages

3. Bands of color or pattern in weft

4. Blocks of color, texture, or pattern

5. Freeform shapes

A.4B. Warp design possibilities for spiral top that can be translated into pattern weaves. Experiment with many placements of design areas by drawing ideas on the paper patterns and folding to see how they fit together. Then refine the design.

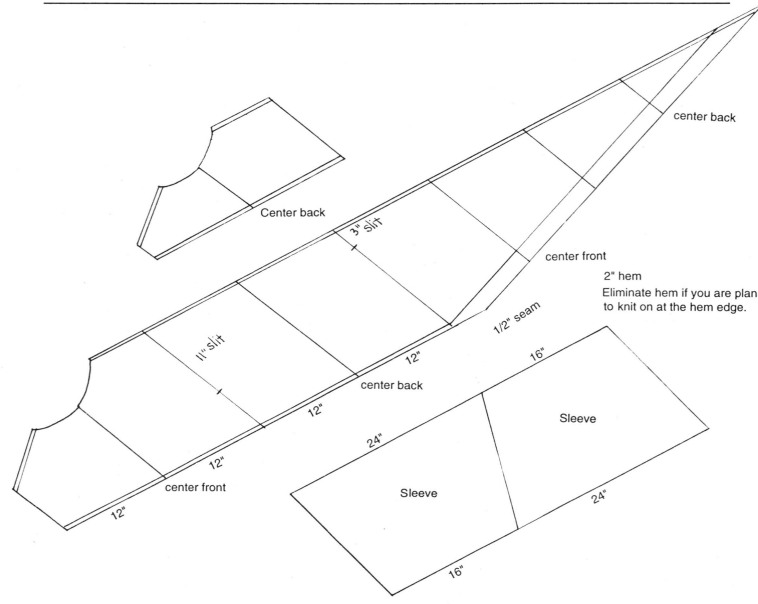

center back

Center back

3" slit

center front

2" hem
Eliminate hem if you are plan
to knit on at the hem edge.

11" slit

1/2" seam

12"

16"

center back

12"

Sleeve

24"

12"

center front

Sleeve

24"

12"

16"

A.4C. Spiral pattern. *Add 1/2" seam allowance on each selvage edge, including back top piece, shoulder seams and neckline, but* not *armhole seam.*

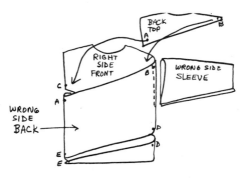

A.4D. Spiral top diagram.

Wash and dry the fabric as you did in your preliminary sample. If you are using a machine, take special care that this long strip does not become caught around the agitator. (You could add several large towels to the load.) Check frequently during the wash time and finish by pressing as desired. It is best to press the fabric on the wrong side. Pin the full size pattern (which you have enlarged from the directions given) onto the fabric. Cut and finish the cut edges immediately with a running zigzag or by using a serger. (You should be able to cut handwoven cloth without having to stitch first along cutting lines before cutting.) In rare cases, this may be necessary, but your fabric should be sufficiently stable to cut without taking this precaution (Figs. A.4C and D).

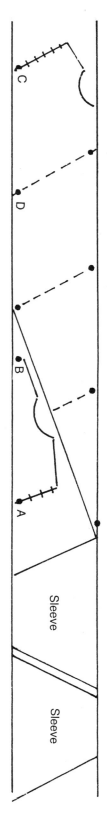

A.4E. Pattern layout on warp.

Assembling the Top

Step 1. Sew upper back to selvage edge.

Match dots at A-A and B-B. Pin upper back to selvage edge right sides together. See Figure A.4A.

Step 2. The Spiral Seam

Match dots A and C, D and D, and E and E, right sides together, forming a tube. Pin and check match at center front and back. Stitch, starting at A-C, ending at E-E. See Fig. A.4E.

Step 3. Measure 11" down from front shoulder seam line. (This measurement should be 1/2 of the finished sleeve width at the top.) Mark a line with chalk or thread for an armhole slit. Repeat for other side. At the lower end of each line, reinforce with machine stitching, using smaller stitches at the bottom of the slash line. Tapering the stitching line as you approach the bottom of the slash, rotate fabric with needle down, take two or three stitches across the base of the slash line, leave needle down, rotate cloth again and stitch up other side. Slash to the reinforced point. Finish the slashed edges with zigzag. See Fig. A.4F. Reinforce the 11" slit for sleeve, slash to point. Reinforce 3" slit for sleeve, slash to point.

Step 4. Sew shoulder seams, right sides of fabric together with 5/8" seam.

Step 5. Sew underarm seams of sleeves, right sides of fabric together.

Step 6. Match shoulder seam with shoulder dot, match underarm seam with stitching at the end point of the slash (right sides together). Stitch a 1/2" seam, but where the reinforcement stitching begins to taper, the sleeve seam allowance will remain 1/2", while the stitching line will follow the reinforcement stitching.

Step 7. Serge or zigzag armhole seam edges together and press toward the sleeve.

Step 8. Finish the neck by one of the following:
1) knit ribbing
2) turn under edge and hem
3) cut facing from extra fabric

Step 9.
Hem sleeves and lower edge, or finish by knitting.

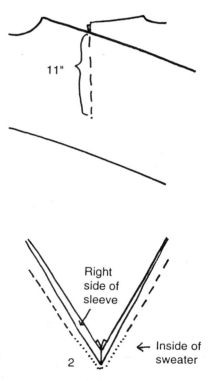

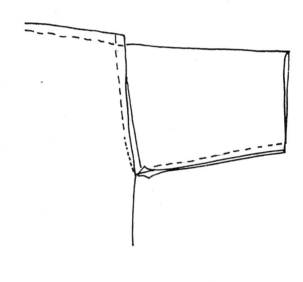

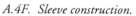

A.4F. Sleeve construction.
1. Mark a line for a slit 11" down from shoulder seam.
2. Do reinforcement stitching around point of slit before cutting. Make stitches closer to the last 1" of slit; make 2-3 stitches across end of slit.
3. Do reinforcement stitching 1/2" from edge of sleeve.

Notes

The neck piece is cut 1 1/2" longer than the front so that the shoulder seam lies properly. The pattern can be reversed so that the front has two seams instead of the back, by recutting the neck and back pieces to fit; that is, on present front neck and shoulder seams, add 1 1/2" and cut neck more shallow. On present back piece and shoulder seams, remove 1 1/2" and cut neck deeper.

You can experiment with different warp widths and sizes. A narrower warp can result in a shorter sweater. Increase width by increasing the 12" section to 12 1/2", 13" or more inches. Decrease width by reducing that measurement. The angle of the center front line depends on the width of the stripes and the size of the sections. To establish the angle of the center front line, find the crosswise grain line. Divide the size of the section in half. Following Fig. A.4G, draft the angle which will be repeated for side seam lines and center back line. To establish the slanting line for the hem, place a straightedge between seam allowance dots on side fold lines (Fig. A.4H). A hem can be added. The back piece must be increased or decreased proportionally. When a narrower warp is used, the width may not be acceptable as the sleeve length. This experimenting should first be tried out in muslin before beginning to weave.

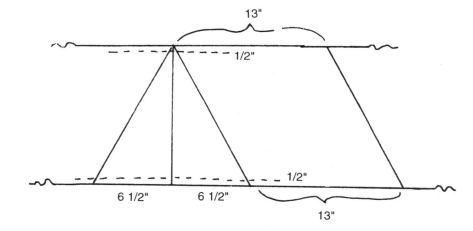

A.4C. Establishing the angle of the center front line.

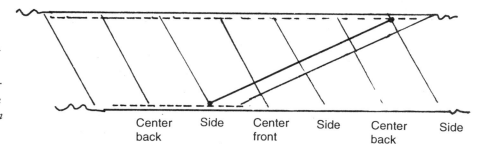

A.4H. To establish the slanting line for hem, place a straightedge between seam allowance dots on side fold lines. A hem can be added.

Starting with a pale beige or white yarn:

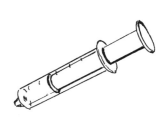

1. Obtain very large hypodermic needles from a veterinarian (he or she will cut off the needle ends), or purchase dye syringes from a dye supplier.

2. Wet yarn thoroughly and squeeze out all extra water. Mix dyes according to package instructions. (I use Cushing dyes.) Dilute colors to desired strength. Preheat oven to 300° for wool and 175-200° for silk.

3. Lay the dampened yarns on newspapers. Dip syringes into dyes and inject colors on yarns where you wish. The colors will stay where placed and if you want them blended, squeeze the yarn and the colors will run together. (Use rubber gloves at all times.)

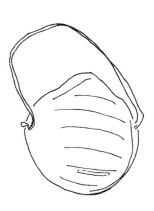

4. Put enough warm water in an enamel roasting pan to just cover bottom of pan and place yarns carefully in pan. Cover and bake for 15 minutes. Then add 1 teaspoon vinegar to 1 ounce yarn. If dyeing silk, use 1 teaspoon salt to 1 ounce fiber. Bake covered for 15 minutes more.

5. Rinse in very hot water, gradually reducing water temperature to room temperature or empty into sink and let cool to room temperature before starting to rinse, as you do not want to shock the fibers. Use fabric softener in final rinse.

Note: Be sure to follow all instructions and precautions provided by dye manufacturers and use proper equipment.

The following is a method to extend one section of a warp, such as for the scarf attachment on Isa's coat.

Wind the threads for the 9" wide scarf section about 3 yards longer than the remainder of the coat warp. Tie on a different colored yarn to mark where the coat length ends and the extra length begins.

If you have a standard warp beam, attach cords the length of the scarf extension to your back beam rod in the area where the rest of the coat warp will be tied on. Use enough cords to accommodate the width of the main warp. Attach the scarf warp extension (the longer warp section) directly to the back beam rod. Roll the extension until it is the same length as the main warp. Then attach the main warp to the cords and roll on the remainder of the warp. See Fig. A.6.

In warping from front to back, dent the entire warp. Thread the 9" section first through the reed and heddles and wind it on until you have wound on the extra yardage. Dent and thread the balance of the warp and wind on.

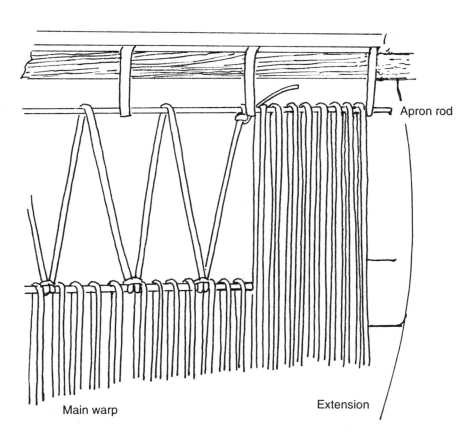

A.6. Warp extension attached to back beam of loom.

Apron rod

Main warp

Extension

To thread the loom for shaft switching:

Thread 1 – Thread through harness 4.

Note: Leave empty heddles on both harness 1 and 2 for each floating thread.

Thread 2 – Do not thread through any heddle. Pass thread *between* empty heddles on harnesses 1 and 2.

Thread 3 – Thread through harness 3.

Thread 4 – Do not thread through any heddle. Pass thread *between* empty heddles on harnesses 1 and 2.

Repeat as above and attach the "floating" threads to the desired heddle on harness 1 or 2 according to your pattern.

Weaving:

Shaft switching is most often a two-color weave. Begin the weaving with two shuttles threaded with your two weft colors. Start one shuttle from each side. Alternate weft colors throughout.

Treadle Order:

Treadle 1 – lifts harnesses 2 and 4. Use color 1.

Treadle 2 – lifts harnesses 2 and 3. Use color 2.

Treadle 3 – lifts harnesses 1 and 4. Use color 1.

Treadle 4 – lifts harnesses 1 and 3. Use color 2.

At any time you can introduce additional design elements (squares, rectangles, etc.) by means of weaver manipulation. On the kimono sleeve, I used a "meet and separate" technique.

Use two shuttles in the same shed. Weft color 1 passes from left, weft color 2 passes from right. At the meeting point, bring both shuttles to the surface, change sheds, interlock wefts, and return each shuttle to its own side (Fig. A.7C).

Diagonal lines can be formed by interlocking the two wefts at intervals two warp ends apart (Fig. A.7D). A steeper diagonal is obtained by interlocking wefts at one warp-end intervals.

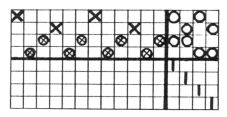

O = empty heddles

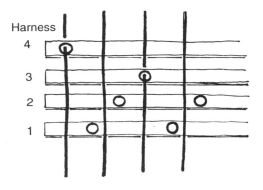

A7A. Draft and tieup.

Harness

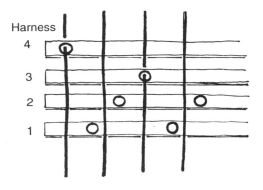

A7B. Threading for shaft switching. Floating threads are attached to either harness 1 or 2 during weaving.

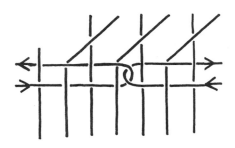

A.7C. Interlocked wefts in the "meet and separate" technique.

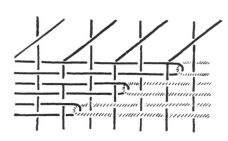

A7D. Forming a diagonal line in the "meet-and-separate" technique.

A8A. Blending yarns in knitting.

Blending Yarns to Coordinate Trims and Woven Fabrics

A knit trim on a woven fabric often looks unrelated, even if the same yarns are used because the differences in the textures reflect the light differently. To achieve a harmonious blending of trim with a garment, it may be useful to work with a blend of the yarns used in the weaving. This helps the matching of knitted, crocheted or stitched embellishments.

When choosing yarns to knit onto woven fabric, a solid color will work if the color appears unmixed in the weavings,, that is, if the warp and weft are the same color. In the case of mixed colors, the way color mixes on the loom make a single color of ribbing seem too saturated or too light or dark in value.

Sample color for knit or crochet trims by selecting and mixing strands of the yarns used in the weaving until the sample matches or complements the fabric. Fig. A8A. This is especially important if yarns were blended randomly in the weaving, as described on page 14.

Using one or two contrasting colors in a knitted ribbing is an effective way to relate the woven fabric and the knitting more closely; or try an unusual knitting stitch that will emphasize or relate to the weave texture instead of the conventional 1/1 or 2/2 ribbing.

The knit portions can be embellished in the same way as the woven fabric, with embroidery, for example.

Picking Up Stitches

Reinforce fabric. The cut edge of the woven fabric must first be machine-stitched several times to prevent ravelling. A serger is particularly good for this purpose.

Sample. Be sure to work a gauge sample with the blend of yarns selected to determine the stitch size and appearance. With the sample of ribbing relaxed, note the number of stitches per inch. This is the number of stitches to pick up in each woven inch of fabric. (See next page for variations.)

Pick up. Pick up stitches about 1/4" from the fabric's edge. Hold your yarn supply behind the fabric. Fig. A8B shows the steps.

Insert the knitting needle into the fabric from front to back. Pull a loop of yarn through from the yarn supply to the right side of the fabric and slide it onto the needle. Continue in this manner across the fabric and then knit in the usual way.

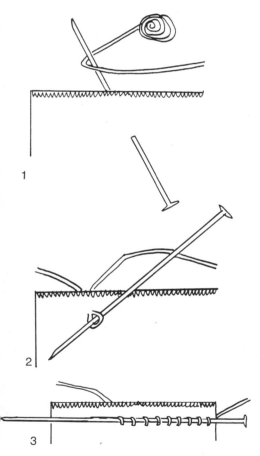

A.8B. Picking up stitches into a woven fabric.
1. *Insert needle.*
2. *Pull through a loop.*
3. *Stitches on the knitting needle.*

Knitted Ribbing

To add ribbing onto woven fabric, pick up stitches in the fabric as described on page 63.

Loose rib. If the ribbing is not intended to gather the woven fabric (as in a cowl collar), pick up stitches in the fabric according to your gauge sample number. If your gauge was 6 stitches per inch, pick up 6 stitches spaced evenly across each inch of your fabric. Space them evenly among the warp threads.

Tight rib. If the function of the ribbing is to gather the fabric for the purpose of fit (as at the wristband) then pick up fewer stitches per inch in the fabric than your gauge (Fig. A8.B). Space the stitches as evenly as possible. This may take some experimenting.

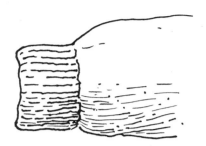

A8B. Ribbed cuff (tight rib).

Cowl Collar

For a cowl neck ribbing trim (a loose ribbing), sample ribbing gauge, then measure the neck opening. Multiply this measurement times your gauge for the number of stitches to pick up. Begin to work in ribbing, changing to a larger needle size every 1 1/2". Knit to the desired collar length (Fig. A.8C).

The knitted edges may be trimmed with backward crochet for a decorative edging. (See page 65.)

A8C. Cowl collar (loose rib).

Backward Crochet Edging

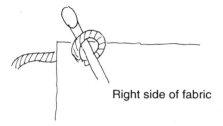

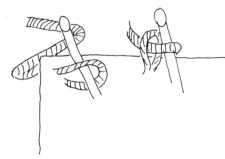

Right side of fabric

Starting at the left side with the fabric's correct side facing you, hold the yarn supply behind the fabric.

1. Insert crochet hook and pull a loop of yarn through.

2. Reinsert hook into material's correct side and bring up a loop of yarn. Yarn over the hook as in single crochet and gently pull this new loop through the loop on the hook.

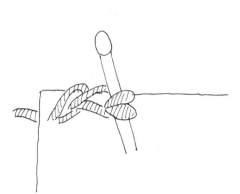

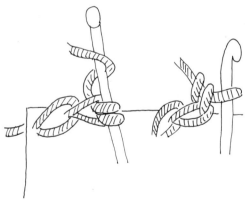

3. Insert hook into fabric's correct side again, and repeat.

Gauge your distances between stitches by feel. Do not stretch or crowd them.

4. Yarn over and pull through.

5. Yarn over and pull through the two loops. Continue working left to right.

An interesting edging variation based on this is to work additional rows using the bars between crochet "knots" as the base for the new rows, always moving from left to right.

Yarn Suppliers

Crystal Palace Yarns
3006 San Pablo Avenue
Berkeley, CA 95702

Eaton Yarns
P. O. Box 665
Tarrytown, NY 10591

Fibre Crafts
38 Centre Street
Clinton, NJ 08809

Halcyon Yarns
12 School Street
Bath, ME 04530

Harrisville Designs
Harrisville, NH 03450

Henry's Attic
Mercury Avenue
Monroe, NY 10950

Jaggerspun
Water Street
P. O. Box 188
Springvale, ME 04083

La Lana
136 Paseo Norte
Taos, NM 87571

The Mannings
P. O. Box 687
East Berlin, PA 17316

On the Inca Trail
P. O. Box 9406
Ft. Worth, TX 76147

Robin & Russ Handweavers
533 N. Adams Street
McMinnville OR 97128

Sajama Alpaca
P. O. Box 1209
Ashland, OR 97520

Scott's Woolen Mill, Inc.
Uxbridge, MA 01569

Silk City Yarns
155 Oxford Street
Patternson, NJ 07522

The Silk Tree
26727 Ferguson Avenue
Whonnock, BC
Canada V0M 1S0

The Spinnery
U. S. Highway 202 N.
Neshanic Station, NJ 08853

Tahki Yarns
11 Graphic Place
Moonachie, NJ 07074

Treenway Crafts
725 Caledonia Avenue
Victoria, BC
Canada V8T 1E4

Wilde Yarns
P. O. Box 4662
Philadelphia, PA 19127

The Yarn Barn
918 Massachussetts Avenue
Lawrence, KS 66044

Catalog of textile books, including costume, fashion, sewing, and weaving.

Unicorn Books
1338 Ross Street
Petaluma, CA 94952

Leather Supplier

Tandy Leather Corp.
P. O. Box 791
Ft. Worth, TX 76101
(Write for dealer addresses)

Apron: Canvas sheet attached to cloth and warp beams.

Back beam: The upper horizontal beam at the back of a treadle loom.

Baseball stitch: A simple joining stitch, also known as Ancient stitch.

Basket weave: A balanced weave structure in which warp and weft threads ar paired or grouped.

Bias: A line diagonal to the warp and weft of a fabric.

Blanket stitch: A decorative stitch, traditionally used as blanket edging; also called **Buttonhole stitch.**

Blind stitch: A sewing stitch used to hem a folded edge without the stitchs showing.

Block: A repeated unit of pattern in a weave pattern draft.

Brocade: A weave structure with two wefts, one structural from selvage to selvage and one decorative in pattern areas only. Also called **Inlay.**

Buttonhole stitch: See Blanket stitch.

Cowl neck: A wide, tubular neckline treatment.

Crew neck: A rounded neckline, usually trimmed with a short length of ribbing.

Crochet: A single-thread fabric produced by a chain of loops. **Backward crochet:** The crochet technique worked in reverse. **Double crochet:** An elongated chain of loops formed by additional wrapping of the working yarn.

Darts: Small, pointed tucks taken to add fit to a garment.

Dent: The spaces between the blades of a reed.

Douppioni silk: A textured silk made from double silkworm cocoons.

Draft: Graph showing threading sequence through the heddles on the various shafts of a loom.

Draw-in: Shrinkage in the width of a fabric during weaving.

Drawdown: Graph showing the weave pattern formed by following the threading, tie-up and treadling sequence.

Feather stitch: A decorative embroidery stitch often used to cover a seamline.

Figure-8 join: A stitch used to join two edges of fabric by making a stitch from the top side of one to the underside of the other.

Float: A warp or weft thread that "floats" over several threads at a time.

French seam: A method of sewing a double seam so that no raw edges are exposed.

Fulling: The process of finishing fabric by using hot soapy water and agitation in order to mat and shrink it.

Gusset: An extra piece of fabric added to increase width at stress points, such as under the arm.

Harness: A frame which holds heddles on a simple loom; or a set of heddle shafts on a complex loom. Also called **shaft.**

Heddle: A string, wire or flat steel "eye" that encircles a warp thread so it can be pulled up separately from other warp threads.

Inlay or laid-in: See Brocade.

Lease sticks: A pair of slender sticks inserted in each side of a warp cross to preserve it when the warp is spread out to its full width.

Loom: A tool for holdiong warp under tension for the insertion of a weft to form a woven fabric.

Meet-and-separate technique: A method of weaving with two shuttles, each entering a shed from the opposite direction. They "meet" in one row, and "separate," returning to their opposite edges in the next row.

Mock leno: An open weave structure, resembling the lace weave *leno*.

Overshot: A weave structure with supplementary weft floats over a plain weave ground fabric.

Pick: A single row or shot of weft in a woven fabric.

Plain weave: The most basic weave, in which the weft alternates going over and under warp threads.

Reed: The comb-like device on a loom through which warp threads are threaded to keep them properly spaced during weaving, and which acts as a comb for beating in the weft.

Reeled silk: A fine silk thread made from filaments wound or reeled directly from silkworm cocoons

Sampling: A sample weaving done to test a particular fabric structure or combination of fibers.

Sateen: A weave structure resembling satin.

Serger: A sewing mchine that binds and trims the edges of a seam.

Sett: The number of warp ends per inch in a weaving.

Shaft: a framework on a loom for holding heddles .
Also called **Harness.**

Shaft Switching: The process of manually shifting threads from one harness to another during weaving to form a new weave pattern.

Shed: The space made by raising certain warp threads and lowering others, through which the weft passes.

Shuttle: A device on which yarn is wound to pass it through a shed.

Sley: To thread the reed of a loom.

Stay-Stitch: Machine sewing at stress points of a garment piece to reinforce it.

Stem stitch: An embroidery stitch composed of overlapping vertical stitches.

Stockinette: A knit fabric composed of alternating rows of knit and purl stitches.

Summer and Winter: a unit weave with the warp color predominating on one side and the weft color predominating on the other. Warp-faced and weft-faced units can be arranged in threading to form a design.

Swift: A tool for holding skeins of yarn for unwinding.

Tabby: A balanced plain weave, or a plain weave shed.

Take-up: The extra length of warp that is "taken up" by undulating over and under weft threads.

Tapestry: A weft-faced weave structure with pattern formed by many different-colored weft, each one moving back and forth in its own color area.

Threading: Drawing the warp threads through eyes of heddles and dents of reed in a loom.

Tie-Up: A draft or graph showing which harnesses are tied to which treadles of a loom.

Tie-down: Threads which anchor floats within a weave structure.

Tracking: A puckered effect in a plain weave fabric resulting from the twist of the yarns.

Treadles: Foot pedals which control the rising snd sinking of the harnesses on a loom.

Treadling Sequence: Sequence of operating the foot treadles of a loom.

Twill: A weave structure characterized by diagonal lines.

Warp: The group of parallel threads held in tension on a loom during weaving.

Warp cross: A figure-eight cross formed during winding, or measuring of the warp thread.

Warp extension: A portion of a warp having longer threads than the rest of the warp.

Warping board: A board or frame with pegs used to measure the length of warp threads.

Weft The thread woven across the warps joining them together to make a fabric.

Weft-faced weave: A flat weave structure with weft threads forming the surface of the fabric, covering the warp.

Note: See Appendix 2 for definitions of **facings, interfacings, interlinings, linings, underlinings.**

BIBLIOGRAPHY

Clothing

Alderman, Sharon. *Handwoven, Tailor Made.* Loveland, Colorado: Interweave Press, 1982.

Beard, Betty. *Fashions from the Loom.* Loveland, Colorado: Interweave Press, 1980.

Burnham, Dororhy K. *Cut My Cote.* Toronto: Royal Ontario Museum, 1973.

Karjala, Beth. *Bevy of Embellishments.* St. Paul, Minnesota: Dos Tejedoras 1990.

Mayer, Anita. *Clothing From The Hands That Weave.* Loveland, Colorado: Interweave Press, 1984.

_____. *Handwoven Clothing Felted to Wear.* Coupeville, Washington: Shuttlecraft Books, 1988 .

Perry, Patricia, ed. *The Vogue Sewing Book.* New York: Vogue Patterns, 1970.

Weaving Techniques.

Davison, Marguerite. *A Handweaver's Pattern Book.* Published by the author, 1950.

Keasbey, Doramay. *Pattern Devices for Handweavers.* Bethesda Maryland: Published by the author, 1981.

Kolander, Cheryl. *A Silk Worker's Notebook.* Loveland, Colorado: Interweave Press, 1985.

Rowe, Ann P. *Warp Patterned Weaves of the Andes.* Washington, D.C.: The Textile Museum, 1977.

Russell, Carol K. *The Tapestry Handbook.* Asheville, North Carolina: Lark Books, 1990.

Searles, Nancy. *The Technique of Freeform Design.* Crown Point, Indiana: Weaver's Way, 1984.

Sutton, Ann. *The Structure of Weaving.* Asheville, North Carolina: Lark Books, 1982.

Tidball, Harriet. *Supplementary Warp Patterning.* Coupeville, Washington: Shuttlecraft Books, 1961.

Shaft Switching Information

Collingwood, Peter. *The Techniques of Rug Weaving.* New York: Watson-Guptill, 1968.

Finishing Information

Baizerman & Searle. *Finishes in the Ethnic Tradition.* St. Paul, Minnesota: Dos Tejedoras, 1978

Gordon, Beverly. *The Final Steps: Traditional Methods and Contemporary Applications for Finishing Cloth By Hand.* Loveland, Colorado: Interweave Press, 1982.

Fashion Design Inspiration

Delaunay, Sonia. *Art Into Fashion.* New York: George Braziller, 1986.

Martin, Richard. *Fashion and Surrealism.* New York: Rizzoli Books, 1987.

Many of the Dover books, including:

Hart, Harold H., ed. *Weapons & Armor.* New York: Dover, 1978.

Migel, Parmenia. *Pablo Picasso Design for the Three-Cornered Hat.* New York: Dover, 1978.

Erté. *Designs by Erté.* New York: Dover, 1976.

Erté. *Erté's Fashion Designs.* New York: Dover, 1981.

INDEX